PLAYING THE GAME

PLAYING THE GAME

The Streetsmart Guide to Graduate School

by Fredrick Frank, Ph.D.
and Karl Stein, Ph.D.

iUniverse, Inc.
New York Lincoln Shanghai

Playing the Game
The Streetsmart Guide to Graduate School

iUniverse books may be ordered through booksellers or by contacting:

iUniverse
2021 Pine Lake Road, Suite 100
Lincoln, NE 68512
www.iuniverse.com
1-800-Authors (1-800-288-4677)

ISBN-13: 978-0-595-30486-8 (pbk)
ISBN-13: 978-0-595-75325-3 (ebk)
ISBN-10: 0-595-30486-9 (pbk)
ISBN-10: 0-595-75325-6 (ebk)

Printed in the United States of America

A person who publishes a book appears willfully in public with his pants down.
—Edna St. Vincent Millay (1892–1950)

This book is dedicated to Bill Sr., N. Palmer, Liz, and Callmevee. Thank you very much for your "valuable" feedback on our first edition. We are forever indebted. May you someday learn not to take yourselves so frickin' seriously.

Love, Fred and Karl

CONTENTS

▼

PART III: GETTING THE HELL OUT 155

With the fearful strain that is on me night and day,
if I did not laugh I should die.
—Abraham Lincoln

WARNING:

This book is written with an irreverent attitude. If you are vocabulary-impaired, this means that we tend to be disrespectful, mocking, impertinent, derisive, impudent, rude, flippant, and bold—oh, and extremely sarcastic, too. Those who take themselves way too seriously might even say that we are sinful, ungodly, blasphemous, wicked, sacrilegious, improper, vulgar, and/or offensive. Basically, we take the stance of a couple of rude, crude, cocky, anti-P.C. grad students. Our authorial omnipotence is based on the belief that near-toxic doses of warped humor will provide a welcome break from the mind-numbing jargon you're fed in massive doses on your trip through grad school. Throughout this book, we poke fun at the pervasive sense of somber importance that permeates almost every corner of the Ivory Towers. We aim to write graffiti all over a couple of those towers, because we'd like to help you escape the halls of Academe quickly yet effectively—uh, efficiently. Besides, defacing surfaces with spray paint is symbolic (and it makes us laugh).

If you prefer whitewashed walls then do us a favor: buy a different book. We would actually prefer that you buy something boring if you are easily offended, or if a bit of raunch is simply not your cup of double mocha latte. If you have thin skin, or don't have a sense of humor, please give your copy to someone who will appreciate it, or simply burn it in protest. Some of the greatest literary works have been burned throughout history and we would be most proud to become members of that distinguished club. If you hate the term "Academe" then you've invested your bucks wisely. Oh, and consider yourself warned...

Foreword

THIS BOOK IS LEWD, RUDE AND SUPERB!

Who needs to read a book where professors and readers are routinely insulted, misogyny sometimes erupts and cocky white male egos are celebrated with tongue-in-cheek cheekiness? If you are a grad student, or want to be a grad student, the answer is *you*. Embedded in a humorously obnoxious tone, these bad boy authors provide great advice. To put it bluntly, this book is USEFUL.

As a clinical psychologist and professional coach who helps graduate students finish their dissertations and junior faculty get tenure, I've counseled both floundering and flourishing academics for more than a decade. Over the years, I've read dozens of books about succeeding in grad school. As far as I can tell, this is the *first* how-to manual in the genre written from a graduate student's point of view. I think you'll find that it's sassy and fun rather than stodgy and dull—a far cry from the tomes that earnestly profess to help students with their dry, pedantic exhortations. These guys are irreverent and sarcastic: if they offend you, well, they meant to. They're happy to insult anyone and everyone (especially each other). No one flies beneath their radar. Not even me. During e-mail exchanges about this foreword, because I found some of the quips in their book offensive and misogynist, they started calling me PRUDEnce. You should see what they say about their enemies!

Frank and Stein's underlying premise is quite important: most graduate students take themselves way too seriously, and this only contributes to their stress and anxiety. Frank and Stein want you to lighten up and enjoy getting helpful advice in a naughty package. I encourage you to take note of their tone and relax. Get a life. You'll not only enjoy graduate school more, you'll do better.

Simply put, it takes *streetsmarts* as well as book smarts to succeed in graduate school. Frank and Stein explain, in their own quirky style, that understanding the unspoken norms of grad school and navigating the politics of your department, are at least as important as researching your scholarly topic. They also emphasize that you should always be thinking three steps ahead to the next phase of your program. I enthusiastically concur. Being pro-active makes the difference between getting a Ph.D. and getting stuck with a terminal A.B.D.

Starting with advice for people considering graduate school, Frank and Stein advise prospective students to choose their universities well—which means not only getting into the most prestigious program possible but also avoiding dysfunctional departments. Many novice applicants don't realize that the general prestige of a school might not translate into a great graduate program. It all depends on the department itself—you may not want to apply to the Ivies.

There are many topics covered in this book that I haven't found in more 'traditional' guides to grad school. For example, it's the first book I've found that gives the lowdown on the ubiquitous class group project (a.k.a. "GIG"). When you get assigned a group project you need to be wary: Frank and Stein emphasize the importance of picking the right partner and of being cautious about the role you take on. Professors LOVE group projects followed by tedious class presentations. Why? Because they don't have to prepare for class, it requires a fraction of the grading that individual assignments do, and the profs can grade during classroom hours at the time of the presentation. So smart teachers like group projects—and most smart students hate them. This book will give you explicit tactics for surviving the dreaded group assignment.

Playing the Game highlights ways your approach to graduate school needs to differ significantly from ways you operated during your undergraduate years. You can't get through a master's or doctoral program by cramming at the last minute. These foul-mouthed wise guys alert us to the fact that grades don't matter a whole lot in grad school. Forget about trying to become a valedictorian or receiving a *summa cum laude*. Just pass and get on with it. Rules for success are quite different from undergrad life and these differences are explained in great detail. GPA doesn't mean as much as you might think. You can't read everything that is assigned and you shouldn't try. Finishing quickly is 90 percent of the game. Frank and Stein focus more on just getting out of graduate school than preparing yourself to go into academia—but this is still a savvy approach. Most students who get stuck are trying to write the perfect dissertation rather than a passable version that will help them on the job market.

I'm glad that Frank and Stein tell grad students that they don't need to (and can't) read everything that is assigned in graduate school courses. It is different from the undergraduate years during which it was possible (if rare) to do all your homework for classes. In master's or doctoral programs you need to learn how to pick the most important material, learn to skim, and according to these scatological sages, spend much of your free time sitting on the toilet (their favorite place to study.)

Frank and Stein point out that you should choose your dissertation chair and committee wisely. Yes, this advice is obvious, but it is amazing how many students I work with who have picked their main professor on the basis of scholarly expertise, despite evidence that the person is a narcissistic jerk. With funny (and accurate) profiles of typical professors, the authors explain in detail what you should be looking for and what you should avoid when choosing your dissertation advisor. You've got to dodge inattentive, incompetent and malevolent advisors in order to get out. And they point out the often-overlooked importance of making sure your committee members work well together. I've certainly seen defenses go awry because of professorial infighting. Do your research and think tactically. A supportive committee is essential.

Keeping your work focused on the end goal—the M.A. or Ph.D.—is the bottom line. I agree with the arrogant authors that every paper for every class should be related to your dissertation project. If you plan carefully, the majority of your coursework, most of your class papers, and all of your work on your comprehensive exams, can be used toward your dissertation. I agree—ideally, you can have your literature review pretty much written before you even defend your prospectus. Of course, this means you need to know your scholarly direction very early in grad school. And you should. If you don't have a clue at the end of your first year about where you want to focus your scholarly efforts, take some time off, make some money and figure out whether you really want that Ph.D. People who flounder about with no direction end up taking years longer to finish (which translates into major financial debt and a less appealing curriculum vita).

While Frank and Stein's specific dissertation writing advice is targeted towards grad students in the social sciences, the advice will still be well-worth reading, if somewhat less comprehensive, for wanna-be-docs in the sciences and humanities. With that caveat, they offer up some great tips for writing and defending the proposal, for working on the methodology section and for pleasing the Institutional Review Board.

My warning about their naughty style, is not to say that the more serious and earnest true personalities of Frank and Stein don't peek out from time to time. They genuinely understand the plight of overworked professors. Specifically, they are realistic about how long it takes professors to read and return material, and they give good suggestions about the work you can be doing while you wait to get comments back. I'm so glad that they point out the pro-active strategy of staying on track while you wait for feedback: so many students I work with come to a screeching halt for weeks (or months) while they're waiting for their advisors to return drafts of dissertation chapters. As Frank and Stein point out, professors have many demands on their time, and you can't realistically expect them to put your work ahead of more pressing priorities. You aren't the main plane on your professors' radar screen.

Finally, and happily, Frank and Stein have found funny quotes to sprinkle throughout the book. I laughed out loud when reading some of the quips they've unearthed.

I teach a class called "Graduate School Survival Skills" at the University of North Carolina at Chapel Hill, and I'm already planning to recommend this book to my students. For years I've been giving much of the advice that I read for the first time in *Playing the Game*. (I don't, however, use the same language. I'm much more PRUDEnt.)

In short, buy this book. You need it.

Mary McKinney, Ph.D. (a.k.a. "PRUDEnce"),
Clinical Psychologist and Academic Career Coach
www.successfulacademic.com

I'm trying to arrange my life so that I don't even have to be present.
—Unknown (but Karl will take credit for it—he's such an ass)

Preface

When we started writing the original version of this book, we mistakenly called this preface a "foreword." Stupid, we know. But that was before we found out that the foreword was supposed to be written by someone else (at least we think so)…oops!

> *On a side note: We've actually gotten someone of importance to write one this time! No really, she's not imaginary like Karl's girlfriend.*

As we wrote the original "preface" of this book, we re-wrote it three or four times. The problem was, neither of us has ever actually read one…and yes, we both earned doctorates from top programs. Go figure. So we looked up the term "preface" in the dictionary, and you'll never believe what it says. That's right, it simply says, "foreword." Even Webster doesn't know what a preface is…With that in mind, our advice is to forget the frickin' preface and just read the book. That's where all of the good stuff is located. Shortcuts are nice—in fact, we love 'em— but you're not likely to find the elusive meaning of life (by the way—it's 42) in a preface (or a foreword for that matter).

> *I have never liked working. To me a job is an invasion of privacy.*
> —Danny McGoorty

Why'd We Write This?

Both authors "excelled" in graduate school. We put in our time and are eager to share our experiences with as many people as we can. We could probably tell you that, as our colleagues sat bewildered and slightly stunned by our "brilliance" throughout our graduate school years, they observed our apparent easy success with profound frustration—but that would be (more than) a slight exaggeration of the truth. It is true that graduate school was easier for us than it was for many of these colleagues, but many of the secrets that are revealed between the covers of this book are things we couldn't have possibly known until we were actually experiencing them. As we stumbled blindly through our experience, we figured out the tricks of the trade while learning to "play the game" of graduate school. Like most, we learned on the fly, and often had to adjust our strategies as events unfolded. Read this book, and you'll be a step ahead, and prepared to face challenges before they gobble you up.

Ok, enough of that crap—the reality is that we cooked up the idea for this book after we graduated with our Ph.D.'s and began comparing notes on our experiences and strategies we had used to deal with them. We performed a little "research" by interviewing other graduates and those who were still in school, as well. According to our highly scientific and thoroughly conducted research study (n = 2), most graduate students seem to spend half of their graduate school career in a confused fog with their heads up their asses simultaneously trying to figure out what the hell is actually going on. Most students spend a lot of time trying to figure out what the requirements *really* are, and what they really *need* to do in order to get the graduate degree they are working so hard for. So, a little more than halfway through their programs, they finally start learning the unwritten rules of "the game." Some take even longer than that. The rest? Hopeless.

Anyway, when we tossed around the idea for this book, a bunch of our colleagues that were still in school told us that it was a great idea. So here it is. If you don't like it, blame them. If you do like it, hell, read the damn thing and be sure to tell everyone you meet how great it is. When Christmas and birthdays come around you know just what to get them. And by the way, if in case it hasn't been obvious to you up to this point, this book is meant to be a light-hearted attempt to poke fun at the graduate school process while simultaneously educating our readers. Please lighten up before reading any further. Oh, and one more thing—seriously, next time don't waste your time reading a preface.

Helpful Hint: Even though we've already made fun of you for reading this preface, we recommend that you read (or at least skim) this whole book **before** *you actually begin your program. You will find some helpful advice in Part II and Part III that streetsmart students follow during the early stages (consider yourself warned).*

Acknowledgments

For the second, new and/or improved version of *Playing the Game*, we would like to acknowledge Mary McKinney for putting herself out there and believing in this piece of shit we like to call "a book." We'd also like to give a special big-ups for Dwayne "hey, hey, hey" from the big WF for having the balls to see what this thing was all about. We knew there had to be at least one or two academics out there who would find meaning in this project and most importantly—GET THE POINT! We will forever be indebted! Well, not really—but isn't that what authors are supposed to say at this point? Oh well, screw it. Now it's time to actually begin *Playing the Game*...

INTRODUCTION

▼

> *Learning. The kind of ignorance distinguishing the studious.*
> —Ambrose Bierce

Book Smarts vs. Streetsmarts:
Are You Even Smart Enough for Graduate School?

Beats the hell out of us, but we can offer this retread quote that you'll find in just about every cheesy book that has ever been written on graduate school. We guess you could say it's an oldie, but a goodie. "Approximately 50 percent of doctoral students drop out of their program. Even those students who have invested several years and made it to candidacy aren't safe—approximately one-fifth of students who attain candidacy fail to finish" (Peters, 1997; p. 9). You might not even know what the hell "candidacy" is at this point, but don't worry, we'll explain it later, but you should at the very least be somewhat alarmed by that statistic.

According to that highly scientific and thoroughly conducted research study referred to in the preface, however, we contend that there *are* different kinds of smarts. Chances are that if you made it through your undergraduate program without flunking out too many times, you have some sort of book smarts. Graduate school (especially doctoral programs), however, can require a completely different kind of smarts. In addition to book smarts, you'll need *streetsmarts* if you want to succeed and get out before Hell literally freezes over. Streetsmarts will save you thousands of dollars, years of time and wasted energy. The sheer fact that you've gotten this far into this book without putting it back down tells us that you've got some sort of streetsmarts.

You're looking for an angle, right? Then you've come to the right place. Let's face it, if you're what we consider *normal*, you probably spent much of your time during your undergrad program screwing around, wasting your parents' money, getting drunk and sleeping late. Hell, when you really think about it in retrospect, that whole two to three hours a day you spent sitting in class sure was difficult, wasn't it? (*note: that was sarcasm there…if you didn't recognize that fact, you might find yourself struggling and offended from this point on*). When the end of the semester came, you started slamming coffee the night before the final exam in order to cram "knowledge" into your beer-logged head—minus a few brain cells, of course. Well, the fact is, that kind of "intense" work ethic won't work in graduate school. It's a totally different animal.

> *Note: Fred and Karl's use of quotation marks around words such as "knowledge" and "intense" also serve as indicators of sarcasm. For added*

"effect," make "peace signs" with both of your "hands" and then bend your index and "naughty fingers" up and down two times while reading these terms "out loud." Come on, nobody's looking, and you know you want to do it…

An expert is a person who has made all the mistakes that can be made in a very narrow field.
—Niels Bohr (physicist)

Yes, Virginia, You Do Need to Learn Something in Graduate School

School. You know the drill, right? Memorize useless subject matter for a test, take the test, and forget 95% of it. Stay up all night writing a paper, have your printer run out of ink as you print it, hand it in a few hours late with a cowering, excuse-filled note, and forget almost 100% of what you "learned." Right? Wrong. Not in grad school.

Believe it or not, however, you actually *are* expected to learn something this time around. Graduate school is for professionals who want to become experts within their chosen field. When it comes to learning, think of it this way: How would you like to have a proctologist (is that even a profession anymore?) who crammed (pun intended) the night before for his finals shoving his fist up your ass? Though we are sure that you probably know someone whom you wouldn't mind seeing receive this kind of treatment, we do not advise trying to get by without actually learning the material while in graduate school. Although grad school's not exactly med school, there are similarities. Random memorization of seemingly useless and disconnected "facts" won't cut it here. Digestion of newly learned material can only become meaningful through careful and constant comparative analysis with previously understood "truths." Let's face it, you don't know everything now, and you won't know everything when you finish—but take your time to do it right and your oft practiced reasoning skills will help send you down the righteous path to becoming one of the foremost "experts" in your chosen field.

Regardless, if you play the grad school game smart, you should have your Masters in two years or less and your Ph.D. in an additional three to five years—tops. No pointless ten-year marathons before you're fully prepared for your chosen field.

This book is designed to teach you some tried and true shortcuts and how to separate the bullshit from the real shit. BUT, we want to make it clear to you up front that you are going to have to work hard. You are going to have to do a lot of reading and writing, and you are clearly expected to learn the material. We can help you make it easier on yourself, but we want to make it clear that our goal is to help you become proficient while being efficient—in other words, we don't want to be the patient lying on a table with the incompetent proctologist discussed earlier. By reading this book (and actually trying to *learn* from it), you should be able to keep your day job (if you have one), get good grades, and still have plenty of time to party your ass off (or raise children, if that's your bag).

I'm Just a Master's Student, Do I Need to Read This Whole Book?

At this point we won't get into a deep discussion about the differences between master's and doctoral students. However, we will ask you to examine, very carefully, why you are getting your Master's. Like your father, we want to make sure you know what the hell you're going to do with it.

We do want to point out that when reading this book though, you only need to read sections that relate to you. (And if you need to be told this, we now know you're not smart enough to be in grad school.) If your program does not require you to write a dissertation or thesis, then skip all sections in this book related to that stuff. If you only have to have one advisor to select classes for you, then skip the sections about how to put a dissertation committee together. You get the idea. Don't make this any more time consuming that it really has to be—unless, of course, you really get off on reading stuff you'll never use. In that case, graduate school really *is* for you.

Learning is acquired by reading books; but the much more necessary learning, the knowledge of the world, is only to be acquired by reading men, and studying all the various editions of them.
—Philip Dormer Stanhope,
4th Earl Chesterfield, British statesman

What Makes Our Opinions So Special?

What makes our opinions so special? ~~Everything~~, er, uh, well, nothing, really. After all, we're just a couple of Ph.D.'s who were successful in one of the top graduate programs in the United States—just like bunches of others. What should make our words resonate is *the way* we went about it. We both made it through our programs quickly and efficiently. The point we want to make in this book is that the quality of your work doesn't depend upon how much time you spend on it, but rather, how much time it *looks* like you spent on it. We advocate quality over quantity. Though we each began our programs after many of our colleagues, we were able to finish up *before* those same students.

We spent less time and effort—and without a doubt were under less stress—learning the material more thoroughly than most others. We learned the system, used the shortcuts, and learned to *play the game*. In the midst of all of this, we made sure that we learned the academic content we needed to know, and learned it well. Along the way we became students of the psychology and sociology of graduate school (Oedipus, 1895), *not* just students of assigned coursework. That's the big difference between our approach and that of our colleagues. This enabled us to become experts in our fields, gain a lot of (ok, a little) highly prestigious recognition, and still enjoy the rest of our lives outside of school.

Having said all of this, if we had to do it all over again, there are things we learned while going through the process that we could have used to make it even *easier*—if only we had known what to expect in advance. All of which have been carefully detailed within these pages. Our experiences are yours for the taking.

Learning without thinking is labor lost; thinking without learning is dangerous.
—Chinese proverb.

Cranial-Rectal Disjuncture

By this time you should be asking yourself, "Enough of this bullshit, guys, so how exactly do I get my head out of my ass?" Let's begin, shall we? The first task we assign you is to relax and realize that graduate school ain't just for the brainiacs of the world (note the strategically placed colloquial use of the word, "ain't"). You don't need to be in frickin' MENSA to get a degree—although you are sure to cross paths with a few of these types along the way.

Hint: Avoid these freaks at all costs. When that is not possible, make fun of
them (see chapter 15 "The Joy of Intimidating Others"). It actually serves
no useful purpose, but it sure is fun.

Just remember, regular people can get through too—*if* you can learn how to play
the game effectively. Many of these MENSA geeks are the same ones we blew
past in our graduate school careers. They're the rocket scientists who are still trying to figure out what (n = 2) means.

If you have at least half-a-brain and you make the effort to follow the suggestions we offer, you'll be a step or two ahead of the other students with whom you
attend grad school—brainiacs as well as regular guys like us. They'll all be stressing out and working their asses off while wondering how you know how to get
through so fast and seemingly without effort (again, just for the fun of it, refer to
chapter 15 "The Joy of Intimidating Others"). Appearing to go through "without
effort" may be overstating things a bit, but some will undoubtedly take your
relaxed attitude and assume that you're not a serious student. Your ability to
work smart (while appearing nonplussed) makes some people feel insecure, therefore they lash out at those who appear to be breezing along—that'll be you. If you
are worried about your colleagues, buy them a copy of this book. If you're not,
have fun watching them squirm.

Definitions

- <u>A.B.D.</u>—<u>A</u>ll <u>B</u>ut <u>D</u>issertation. Could realistically be known as S.C.Y.S.F. (so close, yet so far). In a sense, this is a state of limbo. When a doctoral student has finished his or her coursework and exams, but not the dissertation itself, they are called, "A.B.D." When you find yourself suffering from this disease, remember these kind words, "Shut the hell up and get it done!"

- <u>Adjunct Professor</u>—a part time instructor who teaches at a university. He/she does not make as much money as the tenure-track professors and has no job security. (However, adjuncts often actually make the best teachers.)

- <u>Advisor</u>—Professor who "helps" you select classes.

- <u>Ass-Kissing</u>—Means the same thing here as it does in your world. Though it is rampant and tempting to engage in, it is often counterproductive and NOT recommended.

- <u>Assistant Professor</u>—the lowest level of tenure-track professorship.

- <u>Associate Professor</u>—the middle level of tenure-track professorship. An assistant professor generally has five to seven years of hoop-jumpin' to get to this level.

- <u>Chair</u>—See *Major Professor*.

- <u>Committee (Doctoral or Dissertation)</u>—Four or five professors who help you choose your classes, create and assess your comprehensive exams, read your dissertation and determine if you are worthy of earning a doctorate.

- <u>Committee Chair</u>—See *Major Professor*.

- <u>Comprehensives</u>—Also known as "Comps." Long-ass written exams you have to take that are supposed to prove that you actually learned something in your coursework.

- <u>Cranial-Rectal Disjuncture</u>—Getting your head out of your ass.

- <u>C.V.</u>—Curriculum Vita. See *Vita/Vitae*.

- <u>Curriculum Vita</u>—See *Vita/Vitae*.

- <u>Defense</u> (*n.*)—As in "*the* defense" of your prospectus and dissertation. This is when you try to convince your committee that your dissertation research was actually important (i.e., that it "added to the body of knowledge in your field).

- <u>Dissertation</u>—Big-ass paper (kind of an ugly black book) you have to complete after you are finished with your coursework. The last major hoop you need to jump through when you get a Ph.D. If you fail to complete it you will forever be known as an "A.B.D. Loser." The world is full of 'em.

- <u>Full Professor</u>—the highest level of tenure-track professorship. These are the old farts who get paid the most and the university can't get rid of them. It can take from 12–18 years to achieve this status, and it's the ultimate goal for professors to reach.

- <u>GIG</u>—The G.I.G. Approach to Teaching. GIG stands for "Get In Groups." Grad school profs love assigning group projects. Get used to them.

- <u>G.M.A.T.</u>—The Graduate Management Admissions Test. Basically a test you'll need to take if you're interested in getting an M.B.A. (that's a master's of Business Administration).

- <u>Graduate School</u>—Hell, if you don't know this one, just go ahead and return the damn book to the bookstore. You're too stupid for graduate school. It's official.

- <u>G.P.A.</u>—Grade Point Average: Fairly meaningless decimals in graduate school. However, these numbers may have some meaning in case you are concerned with some awards, scholarships, and/or future degrees. Bottom line:

The rules are different in grad school. (So get over it…in case you haven't noticed, all of your classmates have 3.5+'s also.)

- G.R.E.—Graduate Record Exam. Long test that determines if you're "smart enough" to be successful in graduate school. Accepted by most programs around the United States. Think of it as the S.A.T. on steroids.

- Institutional Review Board (I.R.B.)—a group of people who must approve research studies before they are conducted on humans or animals. Their goal is to make sure that the researcher does not turn his/her subjects into mutants.

- Kiss Ass—Somebody whom no one likes or respects (not even professors).

- Literature Review—the most detested part of a dissertation/thesis (chapter 2). This is where you unearth and supposedly read every word ever written on anything vaguely related to your research topic. If you hate the idea of writing one of these bastards so much, you can sometimes take a course to help you get through it.

- Major Professor—Glorified advisor, chair of your dissertation committee. Your (supposed) advocate throughout your program.

- Master's Degree—The one that comes after the bachelor's degree. The easiest degree. Period. Yes, this includes the one you earned in high school (This was placed in here especially for "Bill Sr." who is apparently way too proud of his).

- M.A.T.—The Miller Analogies Test. A 50 minute test that consists of 100 ridiculous analogies that also determines if you're "smart enough" to succeed in graduate school. Not as readily accepted as the G.R.E., but much shorter in length.

- Methodology—the type of research you choose to conduct when writing your dissertation/thesis. You methodology explanation ends up being chapter 3 of your dissertation/thesis.

- Orals—Oral examination (not by a dentist or a prostitute). This is when your dissertation committee gets to grill your ass about whatever the hell they please. (Have fun.)

- <u>Participants</u>—The subjects of a qualitative research study. If you plan to conduct a qualitative study for your dissertation/thesis, NEVER call your participants "subjects." It might result in your being sentenced to the electric chair.

- <u>Ph.D.</u>—Doctor of Philosophy. Also means Piled Higher and Deeper (overused, but still a classic). There are actually many types of doctoral degrees, but the Ph.D. is the most common, research-based one.

- <u>Playing the Game</u>—Separating bullshit from important shit in your graduate school program. It ain't as easy as it looks. Everybody in grad school has book smarts, but the people who actually graduate also have to have *streetsmarts*.

- <u>Proposal</u>—[1.] See *Prospectus.*, [2.] What Fred apparently does to his committee members.

- <u>Prospectus</u>—what will become the first three chapters of your dissertation/thesis. It is to be written *before* you begin collecting data and must be defended to your dissertation committee before you can actually begin the official work on your dissertation/thesis.

- <u>Research Assistant (R.A.)</u>—a graduate student who is required to help professors conduct research as part of his/her apprenticeship. Also loosely translates to "underpaid slave."

- <u>Second Author</u>—co-writing a piece for publication with someone else. It can be a very useful activity.

- <u>Subjects</u>—people or animals being studied during your dissertation/thesis or any other research study (This term does not refer to courses!). It is used generally in quantitative research and is considered a naughty word if used in qualitative research.

- <u>Teaching Assistant (T.A.)</u>—not "tits and ass." A graduate student who is required to teach undergraduate courses as part of his/her apprenticeship.

- <u>Tenure</u>—when a professor has jumped through so many damn hoops (e.g., teaching, researching, publishing, grant-writing, service work) for 12–18 years that the university feels so sorry for him, that they let him work there until he kicks the bucket.

- <u>Terminal Degree</u>—like dying (only without the afterlife). There's nothing after it. Highest degree earned, you hit a dead end. You're finished.

- <u>Thesis</u>—Pretty much the same as a dissertation—just doesn't sound as cool. Come on, we know you want to say it, "dissertation." Don't you feel cool now? This term can be confusing because it also means what the hell your paper is all about and why you're bothering to write it.

- <u>Vita/Vitae</u>—a big-ass resume that academics show off all the time. Don't believe us? Check it out. Many post 'em online. It lists every damn scholarly thing they've ever done. No matter what you've been told in the past, size does matter.

PART I

▼

GETTING IN

CHAPTER 1

▼

Any club that would accept me as a member—I don't think I want to join.
—Groucho Marx

IS GRADUATE SCHOOL FOR YOU?

Right or wrong, the vast majority of the comments and advice in this book are based upon certain assumptions we have about you. One, we assume that a graduate degree is important to you. Two, we assume that you want to go to graduate school because it will help you in some way: It's possible that your chosen career might offer a significant pay raise for an employee who has earned a higher degree, it might open some doors in your chosen career, or maybe you're just changing careers or wanting to become a professor. Anyway you cut it though, you're thinking of going to graduate school for one or more important reasons. But…the first step you will need to take before *going* to graduate school is actually getting your sorry ass *into* graduate school…

People who like this sort of thing will find this the sort of thing they like.
—Abraham Lincoln

Commitment

Getting in…STOP! Not so fast. Getting into graduate school is important, but there are probably a few things you'll need to seriously consider before you even begin thinking about getting in. Do you remember the old saying that anything worth having is worth working for? Well…the first thing you need to contemplate is whether or not you really want to make this commitment. In case you couldn't tell, the key word here is *commitment*. We've seen a number of colleagues who were lured by the fantasy of easy money. They reminded us of those cartoon characters with gold fever. In fact, if you looked closely, you could actually see the $ $ signs in their eyes.

The main problem with these people was that they never really stopped to consider what kind of mess they were getting themselves into. Keep this in mind. If you smell easy money, then let your nose lead you someplace else because graduate school's not the place for you right now. It can lead to good money—yes, but easy money, no. Some of the people we know who were lured by the money ended up doing just fine. They were the more flexible ones who were able to adjust to the additional expectations that infiltrated their lives. Other colleagues floundered upon the realization that there was actually real work involved. You need to be aware of the pros and cons of graduate school before you make your official decision. Seriously, are you sure you really want to do this?

Note from Karl: I have a well-documented fear of commitment, and I made it through.

We are most certainly *not* trying to talk you out of this. Instead, our goal here is to help you recognize what you might be getting yourself into before you waste too much time, effort and money. We've already established our belief that you don't need to be a MENSA member to succeed in graduate school. Believe us, the two of us are *not* rocket scientists (well, maybe Karl is, but Fred sure as hell isn't). People a lot smarter than both of us have struggled and eventually dropped out of school. One thing we had that these people didn't have was commitment to finishing. In fact, your successful completion is almost entirely dependent upon that commitment. And graduate school is one big-ass commitment. People with gold fever are often unrealistic and tend to get discouraged by the hard work and lack of short-term rewards. While the long-term dividends of a graduate degree can yield solid benefits, the time it takes to experience these paybacks can be maddening to even the most intelligent and/or the most dedicated student.

So we've got your attention, huh? Good. And now you're wondering, specifically, what are the pros and cons of going to graduate school. Well, as we've told you before—you've come to the right place.

When I was a graduate student at Harvard, I learned about showers and central heating. Ten years later, I learned about breakfast meetings. These are America's three great contributions to civilization.
—Mervyn A King, professor, London School of Economics

The Pros and Cons of Graduate School

Like anything else, when determining if you *really* want to put yourself through this ~~punishment~~, er, experience, you will need to carefully consider both the plusses and minuses—in advance. The following sections are designed to help you make the final decision on whether or not you decide to sentence yourself.

The Pros

Well, at this point in time we can think of four rather obvious "pros" to graduate school along with one that's not quite so obvious. Most people are seeking an advanced degree to get more money, credentials, a better job and/or praise. The one that is not so obvious is *intellectual stimulation.*

People who work sitting down get paid more than people who work standing up.
—Ogden Nash

Money. The first argument in favor of attending graduate school is (of course) money. Many professions offer an increase in salary if you earn a graduate degree. In our profession a person can earn roughly $7,000 per year more with a master's degree and up to $21,000 per year more with a doctoral degree. Since we both earned our doctorates 20+ years *before* our planned retirement, in the long run we should be able to earn an additional $400,000 more than our colleagues who never attended grad school—for doing the exact same jobs. Many professions offer even more lucrative rewards for those with higher degrees. You'll need to look at your individual situation, however, to determine if graduate school is financially worth it to you. Though our graduate degrees meant a great deal of money for us, we actually know people who spent more money attending gra‌d‌uate school than they will ever earn as a result of putting themselves through the unnecessary stress.

Heaven goes by favour. If it went by merit, you would stay out and your
dog would go in
—Mark Twain

Credentials. Secondly, there is a certain amount of prestige associated with a higher degree. Although they might not verbalize it, most people seem to have some sort of respect for others who have worked to attain master's or doctoral degrees. We've noticed that, when used properly in business and political circles, our credentials tend to offer us immediate stature—often before we've even opened our mouths. People tend to consider your words with more regard once you have your degree.

It should also be noted, however, that your graduate degree can actually be used against you. As you read through the following examples, pretend you're hearing it in a slightly whiny, sarcastic voice. For true effect, be sure to visualize acute eye rolling from the speaker.

> *Ridiculous Example #1: "I can't believe you don't know how to do this. I thought you knew everything. After all, you're the one with a master's degree."*

> *Ridiculous Example #2: "You earn the most money here, you should do the most work. After all, that's why they pay you the big bucks."*

> *Ridiculous Example #3: "My cousin's boyfriend's sister's cousin has a Ph. D.—I think he got it studying the effect of home cleanliness on academic achievement in Polish American households, or something preposterous like that."*

> *Ridiculous Example #4: "Having a graduate degree doesn't mean anything. I know a lot of dumb people who have them."*

> *The person who knows "how" will always have a job.*
> *The person who knows "why" will always be his boss.*
> —Commencement address at Reed College, 1985
(but nobody remembers who the guy was who actually said it…oh well…)

Opening Up New Doors to a Better Job. Thirdly, the professional doors that ~~will~~, er, *might* open within your career should probably be brought into consideration too. Even if your present career doesn't offer a pay raise based upon your new degree, you might end up with better working conditions or in a job that better suits your interests. For many careers, a higher degree is a prerequisite. Hey, if you have to work eight stinking hours per day for the next 30 years, you might as well enjoy what you do (a novel concept, eh?).

Praise. And, fourthly (is that even a real word?), don't forget good old verbal praise. One or two people might actually say, "Congratulations." Although, this does not seem like much, it is very important because it lets you know exactly how few people actually give a shit about you *or* your education.

> *The test and the use of man's education is that he finds pleasure*
> *in the exercise of his mind.*
> —Jacques Barzun, Dean of Graduate School, Columbia University\
> (you knew that that one had to come from an academic type)

Intellectual Stimulation. If you're at all considering going to grad school, chances are that there is an intellectual side to you that needs to be fed. Seriously. Even though this book spends a lot of time poking fun at graduate school and its flaws, we both enjoyed many of the discussions and projects involved. If you feel like flattering yourself, you can think of yourself in your present career as being like Michelangelo getting paid to draw stick people. Sure, drawing stick people would have been a simple vocation for ol' Mikey, and it might have even drawn a paycheck. Problem is, it would not have been extremely stimulating for him— intellectually or artistically. In much the same way, you might find a part of you that really hasn't been challenged much up until now—your brain.

If it seems to make financial and/or intellectual sense for you to attend grad school, then our advice is to go for it. If not, quit now while you're ahead (at least you're only down 15–20 bucks at this point). There are probably other reasons people attend graduate school, but these are the most typical ones. You'll need to look at your personal situation to determine which (if any) might be important to you. If any of them turn out to be influential, you'll have to do the math to figure out if they actually outweigh the sum of the cons. Either way, these seem to be the primary reasons most people choose to go to graduate school.

> *Ninety percent of everything is crap.*
> —Theodore Sturgeon

The Cons

As far as we can tell, Big Ted wasn't calling ninety percent of graduate school "crap," but in all honesty he could've been. Seriously, graduate school has a lot of positive things to offer, but there are also some major hemorrhoidal pains-in-the-ass you might note while attending. A few of these "irritants" will be discussed in this section.

Commitment. The first, most obvious con with grad school is that it is truly a big-ass commitment of time, energy, and money. In the short term, you will likely be giving up one or two nights per week for classes and even more for reading and completing assignments. The fact is, the time commitment will change your entire schedule. Realistically, you should expect a major shift in your priorities. If you are not prepared for this, life will begin to suck—badly. If you get a Ph.D. in the humanities, on average you'll be 11 years older by the time you put those three letters after your name. If you're in the hard sciences (titled that not because they are intellectually difficult but because they're considered more buff than the whimpier "soft sciences",) you're likely to be five years older. But, there's almost no chance that you'll get to call yourself "professor" until you've put in another two to four years as a post-doc (these numbers are approximate).

> *Note from Karl: I don't know about all this "you can now call yourself 'Doctor' and 'professor' crap…blah, blah, blah.' Dr. Dre has called himself 'doctor' for years, and he's just a rapper (west coast baby!).*

In recent years, many universities have begun to offer programs geared toward working professionals. Be this as it may, you will still need to be prepared to negotiate with your bosses and co-workers to get to classes on time—or possibly to get some much needed work done on a paper or other assignment. Sometimes that means you need to leave work early and/or miss some work days completely. Is this possible in your situation?

Lost Warm Fuzzies. If you have a family, you will likely miss some of the things you have gotten used to doing (e.g., sports, entertainment, changing diapers, watching television, breaking up fights, nagging, screaming at the kids, family vacations). In addition to the family stuff, you'll definitely miss purchasing some of the appealing items of mass consumption that you usually waste your money on (e.g., the latest zilli-bite iPod, entertainment centers, cars that start every morning, decent restaurant meals, classy clothes, flashy jewelry, leaf blowers and cool gadgets that break after 3 weeks).

If you have a "significant other" (80's buzz word), you want to know in advance how supportive he/she *really* is of your goal. This will be important, because a sudden change in priorities can add a great burden to your relationship, possibly intensifying problems that already exist. We met a few people in graduate school whose relationships fell apart as the student necessarily became more committed to school obligations. In the long term, you and your significant other will need to be prepared for two (*master's* degree) to seven years (continuing on for a doctorate) of extra responsibilities. It will always be on your mind. It's difficult to be a loving and supportive partner when you're totally broke and stressed out about the studying.

> *Helpful Hint: Depending upon your situation, you can potentially use this to your advantage. If you've already been thinking about dumping your significant other but are too wimpy to do it, this might just be a great excuse…*

Verbophobia
—Fear of Words

Reading. Going beyond the outside surface responsibilities, another potential graduate school pitfall involves the content. The first time you're assigned some inane reading, you'll begin to question whether or not the whole experience is actually worth it. Whereas graduate school can be very practical and constructive to your career, a good portion of the content is theoretical in nature. Some people can't get past this, and end up spending more time bitching about the readings than they do actually reading the damn things.

> *Note from Karl: I actually liked a lot of this shit. (See chapter 16 "The Longer You're in the Weirder You Become").*

Managing Your Real Job. You can be certain that there will be times when graduate school interferes with your job—for those of you who actually have one. Can the important people at your place of employment handle that? There will be times when work and other things interfere with your graduate school ~~bullshit~~, er, responsibilities. Are you going to be pissing off your co-workers who have to constantly cover for you? Will people view you as the lazy-ass worker who just wants more money? Will the boss be intimidated? Once again, ask yourself, can you handle it? Or better yet, will the trouble you go through even be worth it? Oh, one more thing...for those of you who don't work, why the hell did you even waste your time reading this section?

Money—The Root of All Evil? Graduate school is not cheap. If your parents footed your tuition bills the first time around, you might be in for a shock. It costs real money to go to school, and lots of it. Tuition, books, gas, and maybe even babysitters. If you are typical, then the money you spend on school might have been originally earmarked for something else. Just be ready for the sacrifice...

They're Coming to Take Me Away... You'll definitely need to consider the mental toll graduate school can take on you before you commit. For even the most successful students, there will be times when your thoughts become distant to those closest to you. Believe it or not, you'll be in the middle of something completely unrelated (hopefully you won't be in the middle of, ahem, "a moment" with your significant other), and your mind will wander to something academic when you are trying to come to terms with something related to your graduate school experience. In the "Getting Through" section of this book, we'll offer you suggestions to help you to deal with the constant distraction that comes with your inner thoughts about grad school. Like turds in a baby's diaper, though, the distraction will always be there. Can you handle that? Can your family handle that? You will need to be able to put your thoughts related to graduate school in the back of your mind in order to get on with your so-called "normal" life. Can you handle that? Juggling these factors sits at the core of the disadvantages related to graduate school. Many of our colleagues were not able to deal with the additional responsibility. Their short and unsuccessful tenures as graduate students ate them up completely.

Trust us, we are *understating* the problems here. Make sure you can handle a full plate (better than the old lady in the movie "10" who farted and dropped hers) before you move on. Even though this book is designed to help you weed out most of the ubiquitous (great grad school word, eh?) bullshit (not so great grad school word) inherent within graduate school, it'll still be there to a certain extent.

A Few Good Freaks. And finally, perhaps the biggest con involved in becoming a graduate student lies in the fact that the longer you stay in—the weirder you become. Seriously, it's almost like a frickin' cult. One of our professors actually told us that—no shit. How weird do you really want to become? It has taken us years to deprogram ourselves, and this book ought to serve as evidence that we're still pretty screwed up—if you haven't figured it out yet. Plan on taking a good two years or so to dry out from a *master's* and three to five to fully get all the bullshit from a doctorate out of your system—we're currently looking into a possible 12-step program for this purpose. If, however, you are working towards becoming a college professor, stay weird. The world of academia needs more freaks like you.

> *Note: after receiving some criticism for saying this stuff in the first edition of this book, we considered removing it from this present edition. However, after much discussion with professors and other colleagues, we still find it to be so true, that we decided to leave it in, and continue to offend the few people out there who aren't yet ready to admit it just yet.*

In a nutshell, to avoid becoming too much of a freak, you will need to understand your priorities, keep grounded and never back down—all the while understanding the need for flexibility and hoop-jumping. If you can't work these issues out early on, they will inevitably come back to bite you in the ass later. Just like your dissertation/thesis (hint, hint)—the more planning you do early on, the e s-ier it will be (see chapter 20 "Your Dissertation/Thesis").

To determine if you are ready for graduate school, Fred has included a lame-ass worksheet to help you sort out the pros and cons that you might face. Think long and hard (no, not that kind of "long and hard", perv) then fill in the worksheet at your leisure. This should be the first thing you do. In other words, go directly to the worksheet. Yes, now. And, by the way—if you can't figure out how to fill it in, then, yes—you are definitely too stupid for graduate school.

FRED'S (COMPLETELY WORTHLESS PIECE OF CRAP) WORKSHEET:
IS IT GRADUATE SCHOOL WORTH IT?

<u>Pros of Graduate School</u>   <u>Possible Cons of Graduate School</u>

_____   _____

_____   _____

_____   _____

_____   _____

_____   _____

_____   _____

_____   _____

_____   _____

_____   _____

_____   _____

_____   _____

_____   _____

_____   _____

_____   _____

Note from Karl: OMG! I can't believe this hunk of shit actually made it into the second edition.

Note from Fred to Karl: Eat shit. I like this worksheet.

Note from Karl: Simpleton.

Finally Time to Talk About Getting In

Have you completed Fred's lame-ass worksheet? If not, go back three spaces and do not proceed until you have. Nah, screw that. It really was pretty much a waste of time. Anyway, assuming the pros have outweighed the cons, we think you're ready to think about getting into a graduate program.

For the most part, you need to be aware of the competitive nature of the higher degree. Just like in the undergraduate world, most schools have a "weeding out" process that begins before a student even sets foot in the door. Through the application and selection process, colleges attempt to identify and reject students who they believe don't stand a snowball's-chance-in-hell of successfully finishing a graduate program at their particular school.

No matter how bogus you might think that is, the university probably has some nerdy stat geek working full-time to provide them with scientific data to back up their reasoning (you'll see what we mean when you take your stats classes). Students who drop out of a program hurt a school's reputation (In our opinion, so do idiotic graduates, but that's another story). In fact, the more students a program denies admission to, the higher the standards of the program are perceived to be in the world of academia. Since "admission standards" are among the elements involved in determining a school's academic reputation, the higher percentage of prospective students a school denies admission to, the better their reputation seems to become.

Schools tend to refuse admission to a prospective student whom they perceive to be incapable of success at their university. This includes students who might start a program and quit because it isn't worth their effort, as well as those who get in and find it impossible (for whatever reason) to meet the requirements. Admission committees may use any and/or all of the following criteria to determine a student's potential for success:

- prior grades;

- standardized tests such as Graduate Record Exam [GRE], Miller Analogies Test [MAT], Graduate Management Admissions Test [GMAT], Test of English as a Foreign Language [TOEFL];

- personal and professional recommendations;

- personal interviews;

- work experience;

- their own gut feelings about you and your work ethic.

- shoe size

*Helpful Hint: Using the logic described above, it is imperative that you convince the admission committee that you are smart enough and **committed enough** to see your program through to successful completion—regardless of your prior grades and standardized test scores.*

Many intelligent people who were admitted into graduate school screwed around so much during their undergraduate days that they felt certain they would never be allowed into another school again. In fact, you can include Fred in this category. Fred's G.P.A. during his undergraduate days was so low that he spent a year and a half on academic probation. Excellent professional recommendations for six years of "exceptional" work in his chosen field and a strong score on the G.R.E. helped him get into a *master's* program where he flourished (yeah, right). Though he suspected that the admissions committee might have been leery about his undergraduate grades, a convincing G.P.A. during this *master's* program and a strong personal admissions interview helped him get into a doctoral program that is consistently ranked nationally in the top ten (US News and World Report). The fundamental issue concerning your admission to graduate school is your viability in that program. Can you convince the university admissions officer (or committee) that you'll be successful if they choose to accept you? If the answer is yes, then you're in. Anyway, to make a long story short (or are we making a short story long?), if you can't get in, you're pretty much screwed. You won't get your degree and all of the great things that come along with it—well, don't worry—there's still hope. Maybe one of the cheesy online programs will accept your sorry ass.

Once You're In...

Once you have gained admission though, this isn't to say that you can sit around eating bon-bons. Don't be fooled: this weeding out process is only the beginning. Since a high percentage of people who start graduate school never finish, it serves to reason that the weeding out process cannot be considered complete until you have your degree in-hand.

CHAPTER 2

▼

At best, most college presidents are running something that is somewhere between a faltering corporation and a hotel.
—Leon Botstein, President, Bard College

CHOOSING A SCHOOL

If you have decided that you want to attend graduate school, your next step will be to determine which college is right for you. Since some graduate schools will take anybody (well, almost anybody) while others are more choosey (snobs), your prior grades and standardized exam score will be important here. In addition, the flexibility of your personal schedule and your geographic location will play important roles in determining your choice. Though the traditional schools are less flexible, there are an increasing number of schools out there that will cater to your schedule or specific needs. There are even schools out there that don't require you to leave your home computer very often (or not at all). Again, you're going to have to do specific research on what is available in your particular graduate field as well as what is available within your geographic area. We recommend asking your colleagues and doing your research at your desk. The Internet is a beautiful thing (and not just for porn).

> *Helpful Hint: Universities seem to be creating very useful websites at the moment, because the better the website is—the fewer stupid questions they have to pay someone to answer. Use this to your advantage.*

We encourage you to do careful research before choosing your school. Don't forget the reasons you're going back to school in the first place. In fact, these reasons should play a major role in which type of school you choose. If you pick the wrong place, one or more of these reasons will go right down the toilet. If, for example, you choose one of the many universities that have the reputation as being a "degree-mill," you'll have an easier time gaining admission and getting through school—unfortunately, the downside to this is a lack of prestige. As long as your degree is from an accredited school though (even if it is a "degree mill), you'll likely still get the pay raise you were seeking. If you're cool with that, then go for it. Just don't feel bad when people laugh when you tell them you got your degree from Sally Struthers University.

> *Hint: If you're considering the nontraditional route, you had better be careful. In 2004, some teachers in Georgia found themselves in hot water for "attending" a "virtual" non-traditional university. Apparently, their higher degrees were "earned," at least in part, through "life experience." When the Georgia Professional Standards Commission learned of this, they were not amused. The teachers were spanked, had to go to time out, and yes, went to bed without dinner. Seriously though, some lost their careers because they thought they had found a short-cut. Moral of the story? Go back to Fred's childhood where his mother used to tell him that nothing in life is free.*

Along those lines, traditional colleges will likely require more reading, writing and research. As you make this very important decision, ask yourself how important some of the following issues are to your present and future goals:

- The atmosphere of the campus—does it matter to you whether your classes will be on a campus made up of fancy brick buildings and winding walkways located in a forest of aging oaks vs. an abandoned shopping center in the crowded downtown area of a major metropolis?

- The atmosphere of the department—does a lot of collaboration take place in a community of camaraderie, or do people tend to feel more at odds with one another? You might have the opportunity to talk with some grad students if you have a personal interview. Good time to "get a feel."

- The resources available to grad students (e.g., number of computer labs, hours they are available, research analysis and other necessary computer software, other labs, copying machines, money for conferences).

- The teaching requirements if you plan on becoming a teaching assistant.

- The research and other academic requirements.

- The residency requirements—very important for part-timers who wish to remain part-timers. These requirements vary from school to school, department to department, and should be considered upfront.

- The departmental attrition rate—this might actually tell you as much about the atmosphere of the department as it does about the difficulty of the academic requirements.

- The prestige of faculty—how much does this really mean to you?

- The U.S. News and World Reports Rankings—as with everything, these are controversial. But they do have their uses.

As we said before, be sure to visit your potential schools' websites to request materials that answer these questions and more. You don't want to waste yours or other people's time asking questions that all ready have answers published somewhere.

As far as the influence your school choice has on seeking a better job—beats the hell out of us. Let's face it. If you're a loser and you go to a loser college, you'll still be a loser—though you will be a loser with a higher loser degree and possibly a bigger loser paycheck. For real though, some of these schools are easier to get into and easier to get through than others. After all, there's a reason they call certain schools "degree mills." Ask around within your field, most people are more than willing to share their opinions.

As far as we can tell there are four different types of grad schools from which you can choose: Large "Research I" Universities, Small Private Liberal Arts Colleges, Urban "Concrete Campuses" or Online "Virtual(ly nonexistent)" Universities. Consider what your long range goals are, and then make the determination as to which of the following types is best suited for you.

Research I University

A "Research I" university is normally a large state university where highly sophisticated, intellectual research is the *primary* objective. You can identify a "Research I" school because football is usually very important there. Though we recommend this type of program for some, you still need to put some thought into it. The most positive aspect of these schools is the decent reputation through good old fashioned name recognition. As off-kilter, bizarre and unfair as it might seem, this elevated reputation is often an indirect result of the aforementioned football teams.

You will generally find these programs to be more traditional in nature. Over the years, these schools have established strong reputations based upon the way they do business. Since they have less to gain (and more to lose) by jumping headfirst into risky fads (e.g. distance learning, online classes), they are sometimes slower to change than some of the "younger" schools. Traditional programs include on-campus classes with on-site professors. If you are interested in becoming a college professor some day (or attending football games), this is probably the right choice for you.

One downside of these schools is the size. If you're looking for support, a larger school like this can lead you down a lonely road. The enrollment is usually pretty large, so you may end up working with people in a class that you'll never see again. Networking isn't impossible here, though it takes more effort. Oh yeah, and the politics can be a real pain-in-the-ass too. Since research is the primary objective of the professors, where do you think that places graduate students? If you guessed "lower on the totem pole," you're exactly right. In fact, if you said that it places graduate students at the level of "research slaves," you get extra credit.

Finally, you will find that some of the professors at "Research I" schools have little actual work experience in the field and yet claim to be experts. These opinionated know-it-alls can be quite frustrating to someone who is currently working in the field and enjoys a sense of competence. This is especially so when one of your kiss-ass classmates (who incidentally also has never worked in the field) jumps on the bandwagon and tries to please the professor by making you look stupid.

Small Private Liberal Arts College or University

If you're like Norm Peterson from the television show, Cheers, and it really is important to go "where everybody knows your name," then you might be interested in a smaller liberal arts college. They usually offer *master's* degrees at these small private schools, but if you're interested in working on a doctorate, you'll probably have to search elsewhere. In other words, if you are seeking a terminal degree, this is probably not your choice. But, if you are seeking a *master's* degree in a warm and fuzzy environment, this school might be the best choice for you.

One positive aspect of the small private liberal arts university is the small-town mentality. At a school like this, professors will in fact know your name unless they're too senile. That can be very helpful in negotiating your way through your classes and your program. Since enrollment is smaller at these types of colleges, you will likely come across your classmates on a more regular basis. As we stated before, many students begin their graduate programs with certain expectations, then reality hits. After taking a few classes with a group of people, the connections you make with colleagues at a small college might provide you with the group support to counter the frustration. A "we're all in this thing together" attitude could go a long way in helping you cope with a seemingly inane aspect of your program that might otherwise prove to be your undoing.

There are some problems with this type of school, however. One, private schools are usually very expensive compared to public universities. Financial reality may eliminate this choice for you. Another problem is the lack of name recognition in most cases. Although people in the local area usually know (or have an inflated opinion of) the small liberal arts school's reputation, don't be deceived. Unless you plan on staying within pissing distance of this school, *nobody* will have even heard of it. One look through a database of liberal arts colleges throughout the United States will yield the not-so-surprising result: These places are a dime a dozen. No matter how hard you work in order to earn your degree (and many of them are quite grueling), if you leave the local area, a degree from one of these places might only gain you about the same amount of respect as Rodney Dangerfield.

Urban "Concrete Campus"

If you are the busy, upwardly mobile, life in the fast lane, climb the corporate ladder go-getter, then you might be interested in the Concrete Campus. These schools are generally located in major cities and are designed to meet the needs of people with real jobs who don't feel like wasting their oh-so-precious time meandering through the world of academia. They often offer courses and programs that fit nicely with your schedule if you already have a job you actually like. Many of them offer night and/or weekend classes. In comparison, "Research I" and liberal arts schools are usually less flexible and will often offer classes that start early in the afternoon when normal people are still at work.

The Concrete Campus often features professors who are more practical in nature. Many professors are part-timers with higher degrees working full-time in the field—what a concept! This is helpful to the professional who is seeking to upgrade his or her knowledge. For some reason, these types of schools generally do not carry the prestige of "Research I" or even the liberal arts schools. In fact, many of these schools unfortunately even seem to fall into the category of "degree mill."

Online Virtual(ly nonexistent) University

The hippest new trend in graduate schools seems to be the online university. Although these are actually real, accredited colleges, you don't really have to spend much (if any) time actually setting foot on the campus itself. As a matter of fact, in most cases no one seems to really know if it's even a real campus. We are often left wondering if some of these places are just some guy sitting around in his underwear running "the university" out of his basement.

Anyway, your responsibilities generally include logging on to your computer to chat with classmates, post bulletin board messages, submit papers, create web pages, etc. Imagine that, all of this without actually having to open your mouth! The problem with these trendy colleges is that (at least in the long run) no one really knows yet if they "work" or not—it's too early to tell. If, your definition of "work" is to get a simple pay raise, then yes, they're probably fine. If, however, your definition is to actually learn something and use your degree for some type of prestige, then we don't know—but we are more than a little skeptical.

As these programs have become more and more popular (and more and more abundant) over the past few years, we've made it our business to keep a close eye on their development. In fact, one can hardly go on the Internet anymore without fending off multiple annoying pop-ups offering online degrees. We observed a number of students as they navigated their online programs and complained about the inane "busy work" assigned by their "professors." The majority of assignments appeared to be just that: busy work. The cheesy products some of these students were awarded "A's" for left us shaking our collective heads in wonder. Seriously, 12 year-old children are often assigned more difficult and meaningful work.

Although the quality of work can be somewhat troubling, even more so is the lack of institutional oversight. The lack of face-to-face interaction leaves fewer ways for professors to verify that the student who claimed to be completing the work was, in fact, completing the work. This is sure to encourage dishonesty in some students. For the honest student, this registers as a red flag for legitimacy.

Interesting Story: We know a colleague whose wife earned a higher degree from an online university. To correspond with the professor, she used her husband's email address. Since the professor had no frickin' idea who the hell she actually was, he replied to her messages "To Paul." No shit. This professor responds to the email address, not the student—nothing like getting to know your students.

Though some courses at traditional universities are starting to be offered online, there are grumblings afoot about the legitimacy of online "programs." In a nutshell, these programs will go through some unavoidable growing pains. We simply caution you to do what you can so you do not personally suffer from one of the growing pains. These types of programs will remain suspect until they have been around long enough for academics to analyze their effectiveness through historical perspective. You'll have to use your judgment on whether you believe the program you are considering has met the true long-term test yet. In many cases, it is still too early to tell. For some, accreditation issues are likely to remain a consistent problem. We believe that, not only do universities stake their reputations on their graduates, but graduates of programs stake their reputations on the places where they receive their degrees (ask the teachers who "earned" their degrees through "life experience" about their reputations, now). Even if/when these schools pass the major hurdles, the big question will be whether or not they will be afforded the same status as a traditional degree. Again, it is too early to tell. Snide characterizations such as mail-order-degree are likely to taint these as long as they resemble the old correspondence courses.

Another Interesting Story: A colleague who got his Ph.D. from some online university. Some of his friends like to tease him for getting his degree from "Sally Struthers U." The lack of respect has apparently grated on his nerves. He's actually gotten in physical fights over light-hearted insults made by friends.

We are not questioning the work ethic of the mass majority of students who are seeking a convenient alternative to traditional programs, nor are we questioning the legitimate desire of these same individuals to acquire a higher degree. In a nutshell: If you choose to go online for your degree at this point, then you are, in a sense, a guinea pig. You might be a pioneer. On the other hand, you might be swallowing a lemon. Only time will tell. Good luck, and we honestly hope that your degree turns out to be "real."

There's small choice in rotten apples.
—William Shakespeare in <u>The Taming of the Shrew</u>

But Which Particular School?

Once you have decided which "type" of college you will attend, you'll need to make a decision on a specific school. Depending upon your situation, you might be in a more or less flexible position from which to choose your school. Maybe simple geographic proximity will determine where you'll need to go. If a school is within reasonable driving distance from your house and you're not planning on moving, it might be your best choice. "Reasonable" driving distance is in the eye of the beholder.

> *A Note from Fred: I lived about an hour from campus. During the fall and spring semesters, I drove back and forth after work at least once a week (usually more). After several years of this, it became more and more difficult. In fact, after a hard day's work, just the drive itself can truly wear a person out. To put it in perspective, though, an hour from campus isn't really all that far when you consider that I went to class with a lady who drove three times that distance. Yes, each way. I wouldn't have made that choice, but maybe you will.*

> *Note from Karl: I too, lived a little more than an hour away from campus. Instead of drawing out the process, I chose to take a year sabbatical from my job and move full-time to the college town.*

Other people we met in graduate school moved temporarily from all over the country (and world) to do the same thing. If your choice is not flexible, move on. If you can choose from more than one school and/or program, then you are ripe for doing some more research. We know, we know, research is a bad word, right? Well, if you're planning on going to graduate school, get used to it. So which university should you choose? How do you know which one is better than the next or which one might serve your needs best? As you will soon learn, terms like "better" or "best" are very subjective. If you are looking for someone to tell you exactly what to do…sorry…Ain't gonna' happen.

There are some pretty good resources out there that can furnish you with information to help you decide which universities are the best matches for your situation and goals. At the moment, however, the Internet is the fastest way. First, we recommend that you look up the U.S. News and World Report annual graduate school rankings. Like all advice (including our own), these rankings need to be taken with a grain of salt. They, like everything else in academia, are highly criticized and up for debate.

Regardless, we recommend that you use U.S. News and World Report as a starting point. Once you find some entry information, you can conduct your own in-depth research if you feel the need or desire. There are several ways you can gain access to The U.S. News and World Report graduate school rankings. First, a free website is available with some of the basic rankings and statistics. The Internet address is: (www.usnews. com/usnews/edu/grad/rankings/rankindex.htm). For about ten bucks, you can get the premium online edition or the traditional hardcopy edition of these rankings. These include a directory of more than 1,000 programs featuring admissions statistics, information on cost, financial aid data and admissions deadlines. They also provide you with in-depth ranking tables to compare schools on numerous attributes, such as acceptance rate, test scores of entering students and reputation. Overall, the access to more data, personalization tools and discipline-specific articles are likely to help you make your choice more wisely.

CHAPTER 3

▼

After rejection—misery, then thoughts of revenge, and finally,
oh well, another try elsewhere.
—Mason Cooley

THE APPLICATION PROCESS

Once you have determined which type of school and which specific school is likely to best meet your needs, the hoop-jumping really begins and this book begins to actually make sense. The next step is to figure out what you actually need to do to get accepted into the college, department and program of your choice. A great place to start is with the university's website. If you don't know your school's web address, go to http://www.yahoo.com, http://www.google.com, or some other Internet search engine and conduct a search. As educational institutions, university websites have their own designations. Their official website should end with the extension ".edu" instead of the more typical ".com". The .edu stands for educational institution.

> *Helpful Hint: In case you didn't figure this out yet, if you do not under-*
> *stand the Internet stuff we are describing here, you should have already*
> *eliminated the online university option (and crawled back into your cave).*

If the prospective university's website is any good, it will have links for you to find applications, degree requirements and financial aide. Most of your questions can be answered here, often in a section labeled "Frequently Asked Questions (FAQ)." If, however, you prefer speaking on the telephone to a human, we wish you the best of luck. Phone numbers are notoriously difficult to find on college websites.

The Application

Much of the application process will be simply filling in boxes, making the appropriate arrangements to get transcripts and test scores off to the admissions department, and obtaining letters of recommendations. In addition though, most decent graduate programs require some sort of writing piece that they can review prior to your interview. This is your precursor to actual scholarly writing (unlike this piece of shit that we like to call "a book" that you're reading now). Depending upon your school and/or your program, you might be asked to review your favorite scholarly article, you might be asked to prepare an essay on something relevant or important to your field, and/or you might even be required to write an autobiography.

Our advice: Keep it simple—do NOT try to impress the admissions committee with self-importance, big words, and too much jargon from your field. Don't waste time describing how intelligent you are, your grades and test scores will already say that. We recommend that you tell the committee what you are interested in getting out of graduate school. Include a description of how ambitious you are and what your future plans entail. Don't overstate your ambitions, yet make sure that you communicate your dedication to successfully complete their program with a long term plan to make the program proud of their future graduate. Solid communication (rather than convoluted bullshit discourse) goes a long way in impressing the right people.

If you can't say something nice about someone, don't say anything at all.
—Fred's Mother

Letters of Recommendation

If possible, try to obtain a reference from a person whom one or more members of the admission committee is familiar with. If this is not possible, you may wish to try an alumnus from the program, the school, or the university. If it's been a long time since you were in school last, a lot of your undergrad professors have probably moved on, retired or croaked. If you are a master's student and eventually may consider moving on to your doctorate, make sure to stay in touch with at least two or three professors after you finish. You never know when you'll need them to recommend you for something. It seems like a simple idea, but it is pretty easy to lose track of these people.

> *Interesting Karl story: During the five years between working on my master's and my doctorate, I lost touch with all the professors from my master's program. In order to get into the doctoral program, I needed to have three letters of recommendation. I had to think of an easy, streetsmart way to take care of this problem. I decided to have my boss write a letter, and then enroll in two courses at the university that would actually count towards a Ph.D.,* **before** *actually applying to get into the program. I made sure to do a good job in each class, and asked both professors to write letters for me. After one semester, I had all three letters, plus I had already knocked out two courses before I even got admitted into the program. Moral of the story: Always think ahead.*

Letters of recommendation come in two main types: Open and closed. An open letter of recommendation is one that you (the applicant) have the opportunity to review before you send it in. A closed letter of recommendation is typically sent directly to the university admissions office. That way a reference can honestly say what he or she wants about you. With the closed letter, it is more difficult for the applicant to manipulate the results. For example, the applicant would be unable to acquire six references, pick the three best ones, and send those in. As a result, universities give more credence to the closed ones. Think about this as you apply. If you can trust a reference explicitly, it might be a wise idea to have this person send the letter directly to the admissions office. Though it might be fun for professors to ruin your life if they don't like you, the generally-accepted practice is to decline to write you a letter rather than bashing you in secret.

You'll hear us say this throughout this book constantly: When it comes to your relationship with any professor, never overestimate your importance in his or her life. Most professors teach a number of classes with dozens, and perhaps hundreds of students each year. It's not that you're an unimportant peon, the reality is that professors have a lot on their plate. Your welfare is not the number one priority for anyone but you. We recommend that you write up a short list that includes your relevant accomplishments. If you are asking a former professor for a reference to get into grad school, you might list reminders of your interests and/or some of the notable work you did in this person's class. If it has been awhile since you've been in school, you might need to take another class or two (at a college that allows students to attend without admission to a program) to obtain a reference. Another possibility is to get references from important and/or relevant people in your workplace.

As obnoxious as we might be, one of the things that we consistently harp upon throughout this book is etiquette. If you are requesting that one of your references send your letter of recommendation directly to the admissions office, fill out the envelope yourself, and include postage. Not only is it the right thing to do, it shows your attention to details.

Nobody likes a kiss-ass.
—Donkey in the movie <u>Shrek</u>.

The Interview

If you are seeking a *master's* degree, chances are that you won't have to worry about an interview—grades and entrance exam scores will do most of the talking for you. If, however, an interview is required in order to be accepted into your program of choice, you will want to learn these few tips. It is our fervent (classic grad school word) belief that a strong personal interview can help you overcome anything…well, *almost* anything.

Interview Rule Number One: Do Your Homework

Basically, know what you're getting into before you go. Be prepared to explain to the committee what your career plans are. If you can, find out who is going to be on the entrance committee. Make an effort to read an article or two by each committee member if possible. It's usually pretty easy to learn the background of your committee members from the university website, but you might have to "Google" them, too (If you don't know how, ask Bill Sr.).

Interview Rule Number Two: What To Wear

Can we be frank here? Don't dress like a frickin' slob or some type of artsy-fartsy freak. If you're a man, wear a suit. If you're a woman, wear a dress, skirt or suit. Some professors will be dressed like slobs while others will be wearing clothes they have leftover from the 60's—but listen—you need to appear as if this interview is important to you. Personally, we both hate dressing up, but that didn't stop us this time. If we can do it, then you can too. Enough said.

Interview Rule Number Three: What To Say

Be yourself. The committee won't expect you to know too much yet. They are just trying to determine why you actually want to put yourself through this crap anyway. Don't be too much of a kiss-ass. Chances are, if you're thinking about a master's or a doctorate, you're probably pretty knowledgeable about somethi g. Just don't go in to your interview as a know-it-all. Try to appear as if you re open to new ideas—yes, even if you aren't. If you go in acting as if you alre ly know everything, they'll hate you. We know that we would. Know-it-all's a a dime a dozen in graduate school (see chapter 9 "The Other Students You'll M et Along the Way"). Our biggest piece of advice is to be knowledgeable but hum e.

> *Rule of Thumb: being humble actually seems to make people think you are even smarter than you really are. We don't know why, it just does.*

Rule Number Four: I'm Also Considering Applying To (Fi l In The Blank)

This is actually the fun one. Make sure they know that you are considering another school, preferably the arch-rival of the one you are interviewing with. Better yet, tell them that you are considering one that is even more prestigious. "Well, I am also considering applying to Harvard, but due to proximity, B.S. University is presently my first choice." The word "considering" indicates you have thought about it—not that you will actually do it.

> *A note from Fred: During my interview for admission to the doctoral pro-gram by a panel of six professors, I used this technique. Remember that my undergraduate grades were awful. Though my success in my master's pro-gram showed that I had the ability, the master's program was not highly regarded in the world of academia. I was confident that I could succeed in the doctoral program, but the requirements and acceptance rate to this top doctoral program were incredibly tough. In other words, I was not optimis-tic about my chances of getting in.*
> *After I was unpredictably admitted and had been successfully taking classes for a year, I had actually forgotten about this until I was at a symposium (fancy graduate school word for meeting). One of the professors who had*

been part of the admissions committee (a guy whom I didn't even remember) came up and shook my hand. The professor actually thanked me for choosing this fine institution over its rival! Remember, this is a program that is consistently ranked in the top 10 in the entire nation, and I hadn't even expected to be admitted in the first place!—It's all in the streetsmarts.

Entrance Exam? We Don't Need No Stinking Entrance Exam!

As discussed in chapter 2, most graduate schools require you to take some sort of standardized test before they will accept you. They use these exams as part of a formula to determine if you are worthy of admission to their little club. If your school of choice doesn't require one, consider yourself lucky. On the other hand, if your school doesn't require one, it's probably not the highest quality institution. Believe it or not, sometimes entrance exams can actually work to your advantage.

G.R.E.

The Graduate Records Exam (G.R.E.) is a standardized norm-referenced test that closely resembles the S.A.T. that you likely took to get into your undergraduate program. Like the S.A.T., the G.R.E. is designed to weed people out. According to the Educational Testing Service (http://www.ets.org), "[It] measures verbal, quantitative, and analytical skills that have been developed over a long period of time and are not necessarily related to any particular field of study." With this in mind, if you were one of those book smart people who got great grades in high school and college, but who didn't actually learn much, chances are you could get hung up on the G.R.E. If, however, you have a pretty strong aptitude and your undergraduate grades sucked like Fred's, you can use the G.R.E. to your advantage.

To avoid a low test score and the possibility of having to retake the test (or outright rejection by your prospective graduate program), we recommend that you go back to the same store where you bought this book and buy another one on how to prepare for the G.R.E. a few months before you actually take it. Other alternatives include your public library, which will have a number of free practice books to choose from, and once again, the almighty Internet. Some good possibilities of books that you might find helpful are:

- *Cracking the GRE with Sample Tests on CD-Rom,*

- *GRE: Practicing to Take the General Test,*

- *How to Prepare for the GRE Test with CD-ROM,*

- *Kaplan GRE Exam with CD-ROM,*

- *The GRE Test For Dummies,*

- *The Ultimate Math Refresher for the GRE, GMAT, and SAT,*

- *Verbal Workout for the GRE Exam (Princeton Review Series),*

- *Word Smart for the GRE.*

In the long run, one of these books (or a similar one) can save you a lot of time, money and embarrassment. You can also access more official information about the Graduate Records Exam, on the web at: (www.gre.org/). If you're too lazy to go back to the bookstore or the library, a simple Internet search of "G.R.E." will yield more than a handful of online pay-per-use test preparations and tutorials as well.

A note from Fred: When I was an undergraduate, I was described by those who knew me best as a complete screw up (that is a nice way to put it). I was on double-secret probation for most of my sophomore and junior years, but pulled it out in the end with a whopping 2.25 G.P.A. (yes, I admit it, that sucks—but who cares?). Having fun didn't help my grades much, but fortunately, I must have learned something. Anyway, after college, I went off to conquer the world in my chosen profession. No seriously, I enjoyed my job and became pretty good at it too. When I decided to attempt a master's degree, my undergraduate grades appeared to be prohibitive. I wasn't swayed, though. I knew I was smart enough to pull it off, and I was right. I took the G.R.E. and did very well. Therefore, a (not-so) prestigious univer-sity accepted me and my shitty grades.

A note from Karl: When taking the G.R.E. I scored the bare minimum in one of the two required sections for my department—meaning that if I had gotten just one more answer incorrect on the test, I probably wouldn't have even been accepted into the doctoral program—it could have come down to one stupid question on one stupid test. In my case, although I had a 3.5+

*G.P.A. as an undergraduate, the G.R.E. could have actually kept me **out** of grad school I wanted to attend.*

The M.A.T.

In some circles, a popular alternative to the G.R.E. is the Miller Analogies Test (M.A.T.). According to the online Candidate Information Booklet (2002),

> The MAT is a high-level analytic ability test requiring the solution of problems stated as analogies. Most of the analogies on the MAT are verbal analogies, and a few are quantitative. The test consists of 100 partial analogies that are to be completed in 50 minutes. The MAT is intended to assess your ability to recognize relationships between ideas, your fluency in the English language, and your general knowledge of literature, philosophy, history, science, mathematics, and fine arts.

Has the word "bullshit" crept into your mind? Enough official gobbledy-gook-speak. In our opinion, the M.A.T. is a 100-question test that is nothing more than a bunch of impossible analogies containing mostly unfamiliar words and letter combinations. In reality, it seems to be a test of how much bullshit you can handle in an hour. Unless you're really good at meaningless analogies or you don't feel like spending half the day taking a test (remember, the M.A.T. only takes 50 minutes), we recommend taking the G.R.E. It's accepted by more schools, anyway. That way, if you're not accepted by your first choice, then maybe some other school will accept your sorry ass. If, however, you want to take a quick test that requires little (if any) math background, buy yourself an M.A.T. practice book and go for it. For more of that certified gobbledygook, you can log on to the following website: (http://www.hbtpc.com/mat/).

G.M.A.T.

Are you thinking about an M.B.A.? Then The Graduate Management Admission Test (G.M.A.T.) is probably the standardized assessment for you. This test supposedly helps business schools assess the qualifications of their applicants for the advanced study in "business and management." As with all of these tests, schools tend to use this test as one predictor of academic performance in their programs—though this test is only one of the factors used to predict your ability to succeed in a particular program, it's a pretty important one.

The G.M.A.T. consists of three main parts; a writing assessment, a quantitative section, and a verbal section. According to the Graduate Managem nt Admissions Council (2004), the Analytical Writing Assessment consists of two 30 minute essays: an Analysis of an Issue and an Analysis of an Argument. The Quantitative Section lasts for 75 minutes, and consists of 37 multiple-choice questions, which fall into two question categories: Data Sufficiency and Problem Solving. Finally, the Verbal Section also lasts for 75 minutes, and consists of 41 multiple choice questions which consists of three types of questions: Reading Comprehension, Critical Reasoning, and Sentence Correction. If you're counting, with breaks and other test-taking factors, that's almost four hours from start to finish. As with the other tests, we recommend brushing up on your test-taking skills rather than going in cold. Some recommended books for the G.M.A.T. include:

- *Cracking the GMAT with Sample Tests on CD-ROM, (Princeton Review Series),*

- *GMAT Math Workout (Princeton Review Series),*

- *Kaplan GMAT Book with CD-ROM,*

- *Kaplan GMAT Verbal Workbook,*

- *The Official Guide for GMAT Review,*

- *Verbal Workout for the GMAT (The Princeton Review).*

This is just a sampling of books on the market. As you can see, the books available include some general books on the test (and test-taking strategies) as a whole, but there are also some that focus on a specific section that you might predict that you'll have difficulty with.

None of the Above

Let's face it, some people just plain suck at taking standardized tests. If you are one of these types, search for a school that doesn't require any of these tests. Some schools will simply admit you with a minimal undergraduate G.P.A. and some letters of recommendation. If you're fortunate enough to be in this situation, be thankful and move on.

> *Not-so-interesting note from Karl: Learn from my mistake. I earned both my master's and doctoral degrees from the same university. The master's*

program accepted either the G.R.E. or the M.A.T. for admission. Since the M.A.T. was shorter I took that (and passed). When it was time to apply for the doctoral program, however, the department would only accept the G.R.E. Had I checked into this before, I would have taken the G.R.E. right off the bat and ignored the M.A.T. all together. Instead, however, I wasted my time, energy and money taking both tests—a good reason that someone should have written this book before I began graduate school.

Throughout this book, we offer advice that is intended to help grad students stay organized and motivated (see chapter 13 "Motivation"). These are two very critical, but oft overlooked components of successful grad school student behavior. As Bobby Boucher's mother from the movie, *The Waterboy* might say, "procrastination is The Devil!" As a result, our advice is often to, "make a stinkin' timeline. It might seem like a huge pain-in-the-ass, but as the great sneaker marketing genius once said, "Just Do It!" We encourage you to make a reasonable timeline that includes a timeframe to accomplish the following tasks:

- Research potential universities, programs, and their requirements online and at the bookstore.

- Register for necessary standardized tests or you'll end up missing the deadlines and bumping back everything.

- Request applications to the schools that interest you AND those where you have a reasonable chance of acceptance. Through the beauty of the Internet, many are available in online forms now.

- Decide from whom to request letters of recommendations. If too much time has passed since your last degree, you might need to find a place where you can take a course or two. If you have had a successful work career, that is another place to get recommendations.

- Research potential advisors at universities whom you might want to work with for a particular reason. Yes, this is something you might want to get a headstart on now!

- Get your resume/vita up to date.

- Once you've narrowed your choices, know the deadlines and avoid the stress by mailing in your applications early.

- Buy books and software to prepare for whatever standardized test(s) you might be responsible for taking (e.g., G.R.E., M.A.T., G.M.A.T., L.S.A.T.).

- Take a test prep course if the books and software are not helping enough. Karl needed to do this for the math part of the G.R.E.

- Contact the proper people at the universities to make sure your applications have been received and completed. In some cases, you may be able to log into your application to see if has been completed and/or what is still missing.

- Research financial aid possibilities if necessary...ah, what a beautiful segue to the next chapter...

CHAPTER 4

▼

The lack of money is the root of all evil.
—Mark Twain

PAYING FOR SCHOOL

This chapter is a short one. We're pretty much gonna' state the obvious, offer you a couple of creative ideas you may not have thought about, and move on to something a little more interesting. As stated previously, graduate school costs money—and it's expensive (there's the obvious). Depending upon which school you choose, it can be a real bank breaker. Since Mommy and Daddy probably aren't bankrolling you this time around, make sure you take all of this into consideration before diving headfirst into a pile of shit, er, debt.

> *A note from both of us: We know a woman who took out loans totaling over $90,000 to finance her own grad school and her son's undergraduate studies. Upon graduation, she now earns $38,000 a year. We are hopeful that she really likes her new job, because any way you look at it, the math doesn't add up.*

We've seen people finance grad school in a variety of creative ways (here come the solutions). Some of them are simpler than you might think.

First, check with your employer. Will they pay your tuition, or at least part of it? You might be pleasantly surprised. How about checking into "continuing education" scholarships? Credit unions, local and national businesses (e.g., Target) or certain organizations (e.g., women's clubs, Daughters of the American Revolution) have been known to offer scholarships in the range of $500 to $2,000 to help offset costs. It doesn't sound like much, but every little bit helps.

Keep your eyes and ears open. Some states have grants and/or scholarships for those seeking degrees in certain fields. Other scholarships and fellowships are available and easily found on the Internet. In addition, if you are a military veteran or a minority, there are certain grants, scholarships, and/or funds available to you that are not available to others. In addition to the methods described above (*not* instead of), federally guaranteed student loans are available as well. We recommend contacting the financial aide office at your chosen university for expert advice and more details (a little more of the obvious, but a lot of you haven't really thought about that one, huh?).

At all costs, try to avoid the credit card trap. Yes, it's true—many universities now accept credit cards for tuition payments. We've known many poor souls who paid for tuition with credit cards. Since graduate school is a pretty long process that generally doesn't pay until after you finish (if indeed you do finish), the credit card thing can become dangerous when/if you start to fall behind. If you're paying with credit cards, it is likely you can't really afford this to begin with. If that is the case, you'll probably not pay the bills off as you incur them. Therefore, you might want to perform a little cost/benefit analysis to figure the final cost of your tuition if you have to add on the outrageous interest you'll be paying. Anyway, the final method we can think of for financing grad school is to save up for it. That method, however seems to be virtually extinct.

As you'll note with most of the bulleted lists you'll see in this book, we've done some of the preliminary work for you. Keep in mind that these lists are only to give you an idea of what is actually out there. If you want to be thorough, we recommend that you follow through with your own research. Following is a partial list of financial aide websites that Karl came across while searching for porn on the Internet:

- College-scholarships.com: (www.college–scholarships.com/)
- Collegeboard.com—financial aid: (http://profileonline.collegeboard.com/index.jsp)
- Collegeview.com: (www.collegeview.com/)
- FastWEB: (www.fastweb.com/)
- FinAid (The Financial Aid Information Page): (www.finaid.org/)

- Financial Aid Resource Center: (www.theoldschool.org/)

- Free Application for Federal Student Aid (FAFSA): (www.fafsa.ed.gov/)

- Guaranteed Scholarships: (www.guaranteed–scholarships.com/)

- International Education Financial Aid: (www.iefa.org/)

- Petersons.com—Financial Aid: (http://iiswinprd03.petersons.com/finaid/)

- Student Guide to Financial Aid: (http://studentaid.ed.gov/students/publications/student_guide/index.html)

- usnews.com—Financial Aid: (http://www.usnews.com/usnews/edu/dollars/dshome.htm)

- Yahoo! Education—Financial Aid: (http://dir.yahoo.com/Education/Financial_Aid/)

Remember, the Internet is your friend. In addition to checking out these financial aid websites, be sure to check out the university websites to get an estimate as to what your actual costs will be. Do the math now, or you'll likely get screwed later.

*Note: This was a nice, **short** chapter. When you are asked to do a chapter presentation for the class (and you will), be sure to volunteer for a chapter like this.*

▼

CHAPTER 5

Confusion is a word we have invented for an order which is not understood.
—Henry Miller

DIFFERENT DEGREES AND DIFFERENT REQUIREMENTS

Chances are that if you've bought this book, you are seeking either a master's or a doctoral degree. Throughout the book, you will notice that we tend to refer to one or the other. The reason we differentiate between them is simple. Though they are both graduate degrees, there are clear differences in the expectations between the two. The terms *"master's* degree" and "doctoral degree" are common enough that we hear them all of the time. Albeit likely that you have heard them tossed around and even met people who have earned each of these degrees, you might be a little fuzzy on the technical differences and/or what they really mean. Don't feel stupid (okay, you can feel a little stupid), and don't be too proud to look over this next section. It is intended to clear things up for you while helping you to determine which degree might be the best one for you to seek.

Master's Degree

So what exactly is a master's degree? The best place to start is with a little history. We wouldn't always start with history, but for this one, we couldn't resist. Read on and you'll see why...According to Peters (1997, p. 110), "U.S. master's degrees began in the seventeenth century as fund-raising devices that catered to people who liked titles after their names." Hey, sounds like one of those "degree mills" we discussed earlier! Anyway, now we know where the pretentiousness associated with some grad scholars came from, huh? Anyway, Peters goes on to say that, "Any student who successfully completed the bachelor's and refrained from ungentlemanly activities while paying college fees was automatically awarded a master's degree." Is that frickin' hilarious, or what? What a total scam! How the hell could someone like Karl actually refrain from "ungentlemanly activities for that long?!" You've got to be kidding me! Well, times have changed thanks to the University of Michigan who began awarding "earned" master's degrees in 1859. (We're still not sure which is worse.)

There are many different types of masters' programs. The list is almost endless. In fact, some of these programs are so ridiculous sounding that you'll find yourself asking, "This is a frickin' master's program?" Following is a partial list of programs you might find at larger "Research I" schools (see chapter 2 for a description of this type of school):

L.L. M.	Master of Laws
M.A.	Master of Arts
M.A.E.	Master of Agricultural Economics
M.A.Ed.	Master of Art Education
M.A.Ext.	Master of Agricultural Extension
M.A.M.	Master of Avian Medicine
M.A.M.S.	Master of Applied Mathematical Science
M.A.T.	Master of Arts for Teachers
M.Acc.	Master of Accounting
M.B.A.	Master of Business Administration
M.C.S.S.	Master of Crop and Soil Sciences
M.Ed.	Master of Education
M.F.A.	Master of Fine Arts

M.F.C.S.	Master of Family and Consumer Sciences
M.F.T.	Master of Food Technology
M.F.R	Master of Forest Resources
M.H.P.	Master of Historic Preservation
M.I.T.	Master of Internet Technology
M.L.A.	Master of Landscape Architecture
M.M.	Master of Music
M.M.C.	Master of Music Communication
M.M.Ed.	Master of Music Education
M.M.R.	Master of Marketing Research
M.P.A.	Master of Public Administration
M.P.P.M.	Master of Plant Protection and Pest Management
M.S.	Master of Science
M.S.W.	Master of Social Work

If you're thinking to yourself, "Holy shit!" don't worry. If you are typical (and since you're reading this book, it's quite possible that you aren't), you'll probably be seeking one of the four most common types of master's degree. They are Master of Arts (M.A.), Master of Science (M.S.), Master of Education (M.Ed.), or Master of Business Administration (M.B.A.). The first three of these degrees have a number of fields within them from which to choose, while the M.B.A. is an uh…an M.B.A.. Hold on tight, there are more lists coming.

Each university will vary, but we have included a list of program fields for each type of degree that might be available at a typical Research I school. Remember, if you choose to go to one of the other types of schools described in chapter 2, many of these options will probably not be available to you. You'll have a much shorter list to choose from.

M.A. (Master of Arts)

Some typical fields in which you might be able to earn an M.A. (Master of Arts) degree in:

Anthropology

Art History

Business Administration

Classics

Comparative Literature

Economics

Education

English

French

Geography

German

Greek

History

Latin

Journalism and Mass Communication

Linguistics

Mathematics

Mathematics (Non-Thesis)

Music

Nonprofit Organizations

Philosophy

Political Science

Religion

Romance Languages

Sociology

Spanish

Speech Communication

M.S. (Master of Science)

Another common type of master's degree is the M.S. (Master of Science). Following are some fields you might be able to pursue with this type of degree follow:

Agricultural Economics

Agricultural Engineering

Agronomy

Anatomy

Animal Science

Artificial Intelligence

Biochemistry and Molecular Biology

Biological Engineering

Botany

Cellular Biology

Chemistry

Child and Family

Development

Computer Science

Conservation Ecology and Sustainable Development

Dairy Science

Ecology

Entomology

Environmental Economics

Environmental Health

Foods and Nutrition

Food Science

Forest Resources

Genetics

Geography

Geology

Horticulture

Housing and Consumer Economics

Marine Sciences

Medical Microbiology

Microbiology

Pharmacology

Pharmacy

Physics

Physiology

Plant Pathology

Poultry Science

Psychology

Statistics

Textile, Merchandising and Interiors

Toxicology

Veterinary Parasitology

Veterinary Pathology

M.Ed. (Master of Education)

Another common type of master's degree is the Master of Education. Examples include:

Adult Education

Agricultural Education

Business Education

College Student Affairs Administration

Communication Sciences and Disorders

Computer-Based Education

Early Childhood Education

Educational Leadership

Educational Psychology

English Education

Exercise Science

Guidance and Counseling

Health Promotion and Behavior

Home Economics Education

Human Resource and Organizational Development

Instructional Technology

Marketing Education

Mathematics Education

Middle School Education

Occupational Studies

Physical Education and Sport Studies

Reading Education

Recreation and Leisure Studies

Rehabilitation Counseling

Safety Education

Science Education

Social Science Education

Special Education

Teaching Additional languages

Technological Studies

Master's Degree Requirements

Regardless of your focus, the first level of graduate work is generally called a master's degree. Though requirements will vary depending upon the school you have chosen to attend and the program in which you are enrolled, you will likely be required to complete the equivalent of 12–13 classes. For those who are counting, that equals out to 36–39 semester hours, or 60–65 quarter hours.

We used the word "equivalent" to infer that, depending upon the program you enter, your might only be required to take a total of 10 classes, with the remainder of your credit hours going toward an independent study (and subsequent paper) called a "thesis" or "practicum." Regardless of what your university calls this exit project, it is likely to count as six semester hours or ten quarter hours (basically the equivalent of two classes). Some programs do not mandate these exit projects, but a lot of them do. If not, you will likely be required to take two or three extra classes. Though we're sure that there is debate over this issue (in academia, there is debate over just about every issue), master's programs that require a thesis might be seen as more academic and scholarly if you want to further your education than those that do not require it. Whichever way you go, we're gonna keep suggesting that you become familiar with all of your program's requirements *before* entering your first class. In the long run, it will put your mind at ease.

> *Hint: If you write a master's thesis and are planning to go on for a doctorate later, consider using your thesis as a mini-study or pilot study for your eventual dissertation.*

Doctorate

Thankfully, Peters (1997, p. 118) also provides us with a little comic relief in our doctoral history lesson. He states that,

> The biggest mystery about the Ph.D. is why it's called a doctor of philosophy if the field doesn't have anything to do with philosophy. Apparently in the olden days 'philosophy' not only dealt with the study of metaphysics, epistemology, and so on but also included the physical sciences because it wasn't clear in the minds of alchemists that there was a distinction.

In case that jargon is a little too much to handle at the moment, it basically means that there is this stuff called "knowledge" and people disagree as to what that term actually means. Some people called "positivists" believe that a real truth exists and the job of academics is to find it. Other people called "interpretivists" believe that knowledge is socially-constructed and ever-changing. Therefore, it is impossible to find it, but rather we create it ourselves. Or as Fred over-simplifies his social constructivist epistemological stance for the lay person: "Bullshit is bullshit because we all agree that it is in fact bullshit." Or "pieces of paper with dead presidents and numbers on them can be used to buy shit, because we all agree that they can be used to buy shit." Anyway, you might be able to see where the "lines" blur at this point between the humanities and the sciences. Very heavy shit—makes you sound like a Ph.D. if you can learn it.

Just like a master's degree, there are different types of doctoral degrees. Some that you might see in a larger school are listed below:

D.M.A.	Doctor of Musical Arts
D.P.A.	Doctor of Public Administration
D.V.M.	Doctor of Veterinary Medicine
Ed.D.	Doctor of Education
J.D.	Juris Doctor
Ph.D.	Doctor of Philosophy (most common type)
Pharm.D.	Doctor of Pharmacy
Psy D.	Doctor of Psychology

Though you might notice that there are fewer types of doctoral degrees than master's degrees, there is still quite a selection of fields from which to choose, especially if you choose a Ph.D. It is by far the most frequently earned doctorate, and is otherwise known as a "doctor of philosophy." Most professors at universities have earned one of these, as have the lovable authors of this very fine "book."

Though different programs invariably focus upon assorted topics, the main focus of a Ph.D. program is to learn how to conduct "quality research" (whatever that is) within a chosen field. You can obtain this type of degree in just about any field of study. You name the field and there's probably a school somewhere in the world that has a Ph.D. program in that subject. If it doesn't exist, maybe you can create one. Really. You can do that. Believe us, you're not gonna believe some of the shit you're gonna see. People study the weirdest things. For a sample of Ph.D. programs from a typical Research I school, see the list below:

Adult Education	Agricultural Economics
Agronomy	Animal and Dairy Science
Animal Nutrition	Anthropology
Art	Biochemistry and Molecular Biology
Biological and Agricultural Engineering	Botany
Business Administration	Cellular Biology
Chemistry	Child and Family Development
Communication Sciences and Disorders	Comparative Literature
Computer Science	Counseling Psychology
Counseling and Student Personnel Services	Drama
Early Childhood Education	Ecology
Economics	Educational Psychology
Elementary Education	English
Entomology	Exercise Science
Foods and Nutrition	Food Science
Forest Resources	Genetics
Geography	Geology
Health Promotion and Behavior	Higher Education
History	Horticulture
Housing and Consumer Economics	Instructional Technology
Language Education	Linguistics
Marine Sciences	Mass Communication
Mathematics Education	Mathematics
Medical Microbiology	Microbiology
Middle School Education	Music

Occupational Studies	Pharmacology
Pharmacy	Philosophy
Physical Education And Sport Studies	Physics
Physiology	Plant Pathology
Political Science	Poultry Science
Psychology	Reading Education
Recreation and Leisure Studies	Romance Languages
Science Education	Social Foundation Education
Social Work	Social Science Education
Sociology	Special Education, General
Speech Communication	Statistics
Textile Sciences	Toxicology
Veterinary Parasitology	Veterinary Pathology

Stages in Doctoral Work

Though doctoral programs can vary (especially overseas), typically there are three main stages in American doctoral programs. They are:

1. Doctoral Student
2. Doctoral Candidate
3. Doctorate

Typically, when a student has been admitted into a doctoral program, he or she begins the coursework. During this phase, a person is called a "doctoral student." When the coursework has been completed, doctoral students must pass written and oral comprehensive exams. Assuming the student passes his/her written and oral comprehensive course exams *and* passes his/her prospectus/proposal defense, he or she has earned the label of "doctoral candidate." At this point the doctoral candidate is often referred to as "A.B.D." This stands for All But Dissertation—so close, but yet so far from actually being officially referred to as "doctor."

Time for another hint: Many students get stuck in this stage, when self-motivation (which is very important throughout the entire process) becomes even more important. A common mistake made by many A.B.D. candidates is to assume that they are ready to move away from the safe confines of their department and seek work—maybe as a professor. Many universities will accept applications from A.B.D. candidates. We say this is a common "mistake" because the A.B.D. moves away from the support system and begins a new phase in life that typically requires a lot of stressful hours at the office. New employers in higher education rightfully expect their new employees to work their asses off to prove themselves. This is often at odds with the A.B.D. candidate's unfinished goal of completing the dissertation. Basically, the responsibilities of the new job override the responsibility of finishing the dissertation, pulling the candidate away from this less important task of...you guessed it, finishing the dissertation.

Anyway, assuming a candidate avoids this pitfall and completes the dissertation, it must be defended. If successful, the student-turned-candidate is welcomed to the club and becomes forever known as "Doctor [insert your last name here]." (Sounds nice, doesn't it?!)

Doctoral Requirements

Although there are exceptions to this rule, it is typical for an applicant to a doctoral program in the United States to have already earned a master's degree. Specific requirements will differ from university to university and even from program to program within a university. Most programs, however, follow a similar structure. The doctoral student is generally required to take a vague number of classes that fall loosely within certain ambiguous categories. The vague number of classes you will need to take before you are ready for the next step will vary from program to program, and within the program from student to student (See chapter 17 "Selecting Your Committee" for methods on keeping *your* numbers down). We'll estimate that you'll need to take between 16 and 25 classes (probably more than 20 but less than 30) on top of your master level courses. In semester hours, that is anywhere between 48 and 75 semester hours, while in quarter hours, that becomes 80–125 quarter hours.

To summarize the three stages we discussed above, when you've finished your course load you will be required to complete written comprehensive exams, oral comprehensive exams, and finally, you will be required to write a prospectus for your dissertation/thesis, orally defend it, conduct the research study itself, and write it up. Once you are finished with the research study and the dissertation, you will need to orally defend it to a committee of between four and six professors. Piece of cake, right?

Negotiation, Negotiation, and Negotiation

If you've noticed, when describing your course load, we've become full of elusive abstractions. Throughout your course of study, you will encounter vague requirements that can be interpreted in 50 different ways for 50 different students.

> *Hint: These vague requirements can also be interpreted 1,000 different ways by 1,000 different doctoral committees. Be sure to read the sections on professors and choosing your committees very closely.*

In the following chapters, we will help you to see how you can use these ambiguous expectations to your advantage through strategic negotiation. Though there are loose guidelines and procedures that are supposed to be followed in your doctoral program, most students do not become aware of them until it's too late. Never "let things happen to you." If you know what the hell you're doing, you become the driver instead of the passenger (nice metaphor, eh?).

> *Example of quality bullshit: Social scientists working in the field of cognitive psychology sometimes refer to the afore-mentioned phenomenon (letting things happen to you) as an "external locus of control." This contrasts with the feeling that exists when one senses that he/she truly controls his/her own life situations. A person who believes he/she controls his/her own destiny is known to encompass an "internal locus of control."*

By reading, perfecting, and learning how to use this type of bullshit, you'll already be a step ahead of The Egghead (see chapter 10) who will be sitting next to you in your first class. Just remember to use this weapon sparingly or you'll be considered The Egghead everybody hates.

PART I SECTION REVIEW

One thing you should learn in graduate school is that the Section Review is a beautiful thing. It allows you to add another easy page or two to your papers, and sum everything up in such a way so that no one ever has to read the rest of your crap—not uncommon when professors "read" your thesis or dissertation. This one is a perfect example.

If you've learned nothing else from Part 1 of this book, you should have at least learned:

- Graduate school takes commitment.

- Carefully analyze all pros and cons before bothering with grad school.

- Figure out the financial shit ahead of time.

- Carefully choose the right school and program for you.

- There are many different types of degrees. Choose wisely.

- Although they suck, standardized entrance exams are usually necessary.

- Be yourself (unless you're an idiot) during your interview.

- There are many different master's and doctoral programs from which to choose.

- The typical requirements for master's and doctoral programs.

- Always read the summary first to see if you should read the chapter (keep this in mind, if you're already in grad school and you've just totally wasted your time reading the last 50 pages).

- Section/chapter summaries are time-savers and bullets are pretty.

Now that you have finished Part I, you should have learned enough to get into grad school. Now it's time to learn how to get through. The "fun" is just beginning.

Note: Now if you had just read this page first, you could have saved yourself lots of time. But, you wouldn't have been nearly as entertained.

PART II

▼

GETTING
THROUGH

CHAPTER 6

▼

We're all in this alone.
—Lily Tomlin

NOBODY CARES ABOUT YOUR DEGREE

...well, at least as much as you do. Remember those words, they'll get you through faster than any of the others in this book. It was one of the first things a professor told Fred when he entered his doctoral program, and he never forgot it. *You* need to quickly become the expert on what is required for you to get through and to get you out—ain't no one else gonna do it. Read our lips: ~~No New Taxes!~~, er, Nobody. Not your advisor, your chair, nor your committee will care about you actually graduating as much as you. Other people may be interested in helping you succeed, but make no mistake about it: Nobody else will ever be as concerned with your departure as you will be—unless, of course, you're one of the idiots everyone hates to be around.

Part of graduate school involves periodic "advisement" meetings with a faculty member or committee. This person (or group of people) is responsible for helping you (and many others) navigate your way through the minefield of required courses while at the same time helping you to determine which "elective" type courses are most appropriate for your interests. Many of the students we knew in graduate school began to feel very comfortable with their advisors, major professors, and committees. Unfortunately for them, many of these students overestimated their own importance to these same professors—never realizing that these faculty members maintained the same type of warm relationship with dozens of other students as well. These students were never given as much time or attention as they had hoped they would receive.

You'll be wise to remember that no matter how close you think you and your advisor are, this person isn't thinking about you all of the time. In fact, when it is time for an advisement meeting, your advisor will likely need to refer to your file to even remember what stage you are currently navigating in your program. No matter how nice they are, or how well you think you know them, they are busy people. Your needs are only one relatively insignificant portion of their many responsibilities. *You* are the person in charge of your own ~~density~~, er, destiny. The faculty will be an important part of many decisions concerning your graduate education, but you need to insist on remaining in the driver's seat. Otherwise, they'll steer you in the direction of *their* interests or what they *perceive* to be your interests. It'll cost you an extra couple of classes (or more) in the long run. That's a minimum of four months time, but likely a good deal more.

A shit load of negotiation between you and others on the faculty will be necessary, but do not, we repeat, DO NOT *expect* others to be up-to-date on where you are in your program, and don't forget your final goal. You are the only one whom you can truly rely upon, and in case you've forgotten, your final goal is to get your requirements completed and get the hell out.

> *Make your plans for the year in the spring,*
> *and your plans for the day early in the morning.*
> —Chinese Proverb

How to Become Master of Your Own Destiny

No, we didn't say master of your domain, and this isn't *Seinfeld*. We're still talking about graduate school. Anyway, it is vitally important for you to remember as you are deciding about which classes you will be taking to make sure they *all* count toward your degree in some way. There are normally two aspects to your program: requirements and negotiated "specialties." Though doctoral programs inherently feature more negotiation than master's programs, negotiation is a big part of *any* graduate school experience—not much different from buying a car. Figure out what you want out of graduate school early, and stick to it (More on this later…). Sure, you will want to take professors' advice on classes, but always remember your own agenda. Why are you in school anyway? You probably have certain things you want to know more about, but in the end, you're there to get the degree. Don't forget it.

> *Hint: In case you haven't caught the subtle hints, you'll need to stay focused on your frickin' goal. Remember what it is? We're not going to repeat it again (that's actually a lie. We'll probably repeat it a thousand more times…).*
>
> *Throughout our "illustrious" graduate school careers, we observed students who meandered through the process while taking a little of "this" and a little of "that," never seeming to focus upon anything. Many of these foolish students (no offense—ok, maybe a little) are STILL in graduate school—with no signs of making parole any time soon.*

Yes, it's true—while meeting with your advisor each semester, he/she will likely randomly flip through the next semester's course offerings and say, "Oh, this looks good, why don't you take this." When preparing to sign up for your upcoming semester's classes, never (and we repeat, NEVER) go to a meeting with your advisor without already knowing exactly what classes you want (read between the lines—INTEND) to take. Like the Rolling Stones taught you, "you can't always get what you want," but if you go in without knowing what you want, you're screwed.

> *Analogy Alert: Graduate school is like running a marathon. It is not necessarily unpleasant for the person who attempts to tackle it, but the sense of accomplishment one feels at the end is the true goal. The experience is important, but do you necessarily want to prolong it? Picture this: you're running a 26 mile marathon, and somehow get steered off course for an extra mile or two. Can you still finish? Maybe, but wouldn't you be kind of pissed if you found out one of the judges pointed you in the wrong direction, leading you astray and adding extra time and distance to your quest? Or how about if you were in the middle of the race and you saw a side street with pretty flowers (or naked women…take your choice), would you choose to go out of your way and run an extra mile **right now**? Of course not, your goal is to finish the damn race, and it's plenty long enough as it is. You can come back and look at whatever you want to later. While you're in the middle of the race, don't let others sidetrack you from your goal (and don't distract yourself either). Know what you want and how to get it. It's as simple as that.*

Mastering the Scheduling Process

The scheduling process actually has two components: long-term course plan and short-term, (e.g., semester, quarter) scheduling. Your long-term course plan involves how you plan to get from Point A to Point B, from initial enrollment to graduation. The key term in this sentence is "how." Once you have determined the general program requirements, you'll want to create a reasonable goal for a graduation date. The long-term course plan sets up what you will plan to do between now and then so you can meet this goal. Your short-term, or semester scheduling plan, is your method for setting up your course schedule for the upcoming term. You will need to continually refer to your long-term plan when creating each semester's schedule.

Long-Term Course Plan

Cookbook Programs and a Checklist. We know what you're thinking. A graduate program in cooking? Though there probably is one available somewhere, that's not what we're talking about. Some master's programs have very little flexibility, leaving you with very little at your discretion. These programs set out the list of required classes in advance in much the same way a cookbook recipe tells you what you need to include in a dish. (e.g., "These are the 12 classes you need to take in order to obtain your master of science degree in psychology from Bogus University"). In this case, we suggest that you print out the list of courses you are required to take, post it in a location that you will look at often (like the refrigerator), and check off each class as you finish it. A checklist of this sort should provide you some small sense of satisfaction. It will become a constant reminder of how far you've gone and how far you still have to go before you finish.

This might seem like a stupid idea as you begin your excursion with high hopes and energy to spare, but trust us, it's a good idea. The chart will offer you a needed sense of direction as you inevitably begin to feel the fatigue and sense of hopelessness midway through your program. The feeling that, "I'm never going to finish!" is as common among those who are successful as it is among those who drop out. You'll appreciate crossing off classes as you work your way up to the hump in the middle of your program—into the doldrums. You don't want to walk around in a fog. Knowing where you are, and where you are headed within the confines of your program is number one on the list of graduate school streetsmarts.

A more detailed timeline, a course plan. To get through graduate school in a reasonable amount of time with some sense of sanity still in tact, you'll need to create a realistic, but flexible, long-term timeline that contains general ideas of courses you would like to take and are required to take. We call this thing a "course plan." Assuming that your program provides you with flexibility and options, take some time and browse through the course catalogue and read the detailed descriptions of ALL courses that are even vaguely related to anything that interests you.

> *Hint: Do this early, and do it online if your university has an online catalogue. You can use the "copy" and "paste" features to create a file that can serve as your own personal course catalogue of courses that fit into your flexible requirements and electives that you might be interested in taking. Do this early, and you'll find that selecting courses each semester will be much easier.*

> *Note: There's a damn good chance that a course or two you take won't resemble the catalogue description(s) in the slightest. That's university life…get used to it.*

You'll quickly figure out which courses are offered regularly and which are not. Keep your ears open while on campus. One of the best times to do this is during class breaks. Ask the most experienced students about this and listen well. It is important to figure out which courses are popular (read between the lines, this means the course will fill up fast, making it difficult to sign up for), and which are easy to get in no matter when you need them (read between these lines, they're probably hard and boring).

You'll need to use your head to develop some sort of simple strategy to get some of the required "popular" courses out of the way. Since nearly every college seems to have a different way to request and register for classes, we really can't get into specifics. But, we are hoping that if you've *really* read this book, that you might understand the concepts we are promoting and that you'll begin to develop your own grad school streetsmarts.

> *Sad, but Entertaining Story: You don't want to get stuck like this lady we knew. She was nearing the end of her program and didn't plan ahead. She needed a specific "required" course that was offered only every other semester. It turns out that it was not offered during the semester that was supposed to be her last. Even sadder news for her, it wasn't offered the*

following semester, either. She ended up having to wait a whole year for this course to be offered again. Of course, she had gone into her meeting with her advisor without a backup plan (remember, flip, flip, flip, "Oooh, this looks interesting, why don't you take this one?") and therefore, the poor lady ended up taking two extra courses. Not only did this result in a waste of an entire year, but think of all the tuition money and other things she threw away for this completely unnecessary crap. Unless her attendance in that class resulted in world peace or curing an incurable disease (which it didn't), we're pretty sure it was a waste of time. Learn from this experience—plan ahead, and go to your meetings with advisors or committee members already knowing which classes you want to take.

Choices. Do I take this class or that one? In other master degree programs and certainly in doctoral programs, there are a number of gray areas. Often, program requirements are split between two types: specific required classes (like the ones mentioned above), and those that are lumped into vague categories. You will probably be required to complete some very specific classes—that part is usually easy to understand, though later we'll share some experiences that we had in getting certain classes waived. The rest of your program will likely be tailored to your department, your major and your specific area of concentration.

You might be told that you have to take "a minimum of five research classes" without any specification as to which research classes must be taken. Within each category, you will find a selection of different classes that might fit the bill. You will end up choosing one or more classes from this semi-structured list of possibilities. These are negotiable. Be *really* careful with them. Learn the requirements EARLY in your graduate school career, study the course offerings, and learn which courses will meet each requirement. Keep reading and you'll find some advice on how to find the best classes to meet each of these requirements.

Hint: Sometimes one course can fulfill two different requirements. Make sure you don't meet a requirement more than once. It will do you absolutely no good. You'll still be required to complete all of the others. If you don't follow this little piece of advice, you're likely to end up going through a lot of extra bullshit and having absolutely nothing extra to show for it.

Do You Like It Slow-An-Easy Or Hard And Fast?

Yeah, baby! [Insert Austin Powers flashback here] Get your mind out of the gutter, we're talking about getting through your graduate program. The question revolves around how you want to do this thing. Are you the tortoise or the hare? Is it important for you to blow through this program fast or can you afford to go nice and slow? There are plusses and minuses to each.

> *Live fast, die young and have a good-looking corpse.*
> —Nick Romano in the film, <u>Knock On Any Door</u> (1949)

So, you like it hard and fast? If you choose to blow through, you'll need to ask yourself if you can handle the pressure of taking two (or possibly three) classes at once while cryogenically freezing the rest of your life. Assuming you have a life, speeding through a graduate program will put most of your extracurricular activities on hold. The quicker you get through, the sooner you're finished with the bullshit. Karl did it this way. He even took a sabbatical from his employer so he could go fulltime. He lives alone, though, and was financially (if not psychologically) secure enough to handle this. Be careful, however, about going too fast too soon before you know what your getting into or you might flame out. Remember, graduate school is a marathon, not a sprint. Even if you choose to go through fast, it's all relative. It's never a matter of days, weeks, or even months...we're talking years.

> *Interesting story: We know another lady who fancied herself a real "go getter." Though she worked fulltime and was married with children, she pictured herself getting through her traditional master's program in a year and a half. With her outside responsibilities, fat chance. She took two classes during her first term, thinking that she was "taking it easy." Her plans were to start out easy, then take three during the following two terms, finishing up in just under a year and a half. By the end of the first semester, though, she was almost bald from the stress—no shit. Though she only took one class the following semester when she realized that she was overdoing it, she had already burnt out. She took an "incomplete" during the second semester for her class (which has since been converted into an "F") and has no plans to return to graduate school.*

That lady flamed out very quickly. Her enthusiasm was crushed and she was unable to recover. Many of the things successful students see as "hoops" were perceived as impossible bullshit by her. Regular burnout can become a real issue if you're not in tune with yourself, too. The question here is, can you finish the program before you're burnt out? 'Cause you're gonna burn out if you work too hard too fast. Can you finish, first?

Slow work yields fine products.
—Chinese Proverb

How about slow 'n easy? If it is more important for you to stay relatively sane during the course of your graduate program, you might consider going slower and taking one course at a time. This, of course, will not guarantee that you stay sane since it will require you to remain in graduate school for a longer period of time—not to mention the fact that we don't even know your present state-of-mind. But it might help.

If you choose this strategy, just remember to keep your eye on the prize and don't get discouraged with how long it takes. Keep going, too. In other words, don't "reward yourself" with a semester break for any reason. Too many people have chosen to "take a break" and have never returned.

> *Interesting Story: In the original version of Playing the Game, we told a story about this guy we know who took a "well deserved break" after he finished his comprehensive exams. Six years later, upon publication of our original version, he still hadn't begun his dissertation. We made some pretty smart ass remarks about this guy in that first book, basically stating that we didn't think he'd ever go back and finish. As we noted earlier, we understand that this is not an isolated situation. In fact it is quite typical.*
>
> *2nd edition update on this individual: with the poking, prodding, and otherwise obnoxious nagging of Fred and Karl, this guy eventually picked up where he left off after a looooong break (see above). Turns out his major professor had retired, one of his committee members had moved to a new university, and we think another of his committee members had actually kicked the bucket. Anyway, this guy ended up spending the next six months putting his "new" committee together, and had to start again at square one with a completely new research topic. Two and a half years later, the good*

news on this "gentleman" is that, yes, he finally graduated! (if only he had met us sooner)…

Another negative aspect of taking your time to finish grad school involves finances. The guy discussed in the story above had to officially "remain in school" during the eight and a half years after finishing his comprehensive exams by paying for one credit hour per semester. Bottom line, the longer you go to school, the higher the financial cost. Duh.

And still one more issue: If you're in the program too long, you very well might begin to forget some important stuff that you "learned" 10 years ago. This can definitely bite you in the ass when it comes time for your comprehensive exams, and for the oral defenses (prospectus and dissertation—See chapters 20 and 21). Consider yourself warned.

Slow 'n easy, fast n' hard, then slow 'n easy again. If neither of the above sounds appealing, you might want to think about a combination. Look at your lifestyle and determine which parts of the year are more hectic and which parts of the year have fewer outside responsibilities for you. If you can predict these time periods with a decent amount of reliability, then you might decide to mix up your course selection based upon when a semester falls in the year. We suggest that you take only one class during the months when you'll be busy transporting kids to soccer practice (or doing your taxes or whatever outside responsibilities you might have) and loading up on classes when your life typically slows down.

> *The favor of a drop of water should be repaid as an overflowing spring.*
> —Chinese Proverb

~~*Beating*~~, er, *Working the system: The independent study.* You're not really beating the system here, but now you're learning to work it—being streetsmart. Thinking back to our lady friend who got stuck with an extra year of coursework, there were reasonable alternatives that she could have pursued had she known about them. You can be sure that the faculty is aware of these, but strangely enough, nobody suggested this option to her. Remember our advice that you need to be your own advocate. You've got to persevere with the attitude that there ain't nobody looking out for you but yourself. Anyway, one of the alternatives she might have pursued is a type of class called an "independent study." We used this option to our advantage whenever we could swing it.

Independent studies come in a variety of flavors and can be taken for different reasons. Generally, this type of class is one that you want (or need) to take but is not offered. You might need to take a class that fits within a certain category that is not offered during a semester that you need to take it (e.g., the unfortunate lady we talked about before). If this happens, an independent study might be your ticket. On the other hand, you might want to take a class on a particular topic, but no such class even exists. Once again, if this is the case, an independent study might be your ticket. Another reason you might choose to take one of these classes is because you are extremely busy during a particular part of the year and are unable to commit to attending a scheduled class. Maybe you can find the time to work on your coursework, but only at odd times. If so, an independent study is a good option.

There are some difficulties to scheduling one of these courses that you should be aware of. An independent study is a class that is created specifically for you by a professor. As such, it can be viewed as a major pain-in-the-ass to the professor. In order to do so, you'll need to find a professor who you know pretty well and ask (read between the lines…beg) him or her to hook you up. If you're someone whom they respect and they're not too busy, they'll probably help you out. We found that, if you are someone that professors respect, they will usually go out of their way to help when you ask. If you're an idiot though, they'll make excuses as to why they can't help you. Maybe that's what happened to that lady, we're not sure. Regardless, you'll want to make sure that you don't abuse this or anything else that puts a professor out.

An unofficial independent study: One student took an independent study in the form of, "if you scratch my back, I'll scratch yours." One summer term, this student's major professor was scheduled to teach a course, but not enough students had signed up for it. Though the student needed this class, she was very busy at this time with outside responsibilities (read between the lines: it was family vacation time…). Not wanting to have his class canceled due to lack of interest, the major professor was willing to negotiate. The student ended up officially signing up for the class, but never actually setting foot in the classroom. She received a temporary "incomplete" for the course and completed the assignments during the following semester. In the end, this "independent study" saved her an entire semester, while providing her with an extra bonus: The major professor appreciated her flexibility because his class was saved from cancellation.

In the first place God made idiots. This was for practice.
Then he made School Boards...
—Mark Twain

How Not To Be An Idiot

If this seems like an unnecessary section, read it anyway. Many of the students we met in school acted like complete idiots. In regular life, they might have been cool (probably not, though), but in graduate school they acted like jerks. Yes, you are paying for your classes, but no, the professors are not your "employees" and they are definitely not impressed by how smart you might think you are. If you treat them like they're a frickin' janitor, they'll hate your condescending ass. Wouldn't you? If you try to treat them like they are your servants, they'll find a way to make your life miserable. At the very least, they won't go out of their way to help. This sounds like basic stuff, but you'll be surprised at the number of students who think that the university is there to serve all of their needs and that each professor should be at their beckon call. Don't get us wrong—most professors want to help—but they prefer to be asked rather than ordered around. They honestly can't control a lot of the bureaucratic red tape, and you should avoid taking your personal frustrations out on them.

Another thing: *Don't show up professors in class*. You are free to disagree with them (we actively encourage this), but don't forget who you are and what you are. You are the student. You might actually have a lot to offer your class, but don't forget that your professors have already completed more schooling than you. Most of them feel that this gives them the right to be "the expert." You might disagree with this, but the fact that they have the authority to give you an "A" or an "F" should persuade you to respect their opinions at the very least. Though you might come across some real assholes, most of them will respect your opinions as long as you respect theirs.

Finally, the most obvious but overlooked aspect of any interaction with people who are helping you is to just say "please" and "thank you." You'd be surprised at how many grown-ups ignore this sage advice. You probably wouldn't be surprised at how insulted professors get when they go our of their way to help someone and all they receive in return is aggravation. With so many students acting like it is their "right" to get special privileges, it is quite refreshing for the professors to recognize some humility in you.

Note: Just be polite and appropriately thankful when someone goes out of their way for you instead of always "expecting" them to do so. Please, don't go up and thank your professors for "a great lecture" or a "great discussion" after each class. That's kissing ass. Whereas it won't get you beat up like it might have in high school, it's still not a good idea.

Strategies for Semester Scheduling

Okay. You've got your long-term course plan in hand, right? You've tentatively decided how fast you plan to blow through that course plan? Good. Now that we've got that settled, we're gonna show you some strategies to help you get from the beginning of that list to the end. Probably just as important as setting up that long-term course plan is how you go about setting up each semester's schedule.

Pacing yourself for the hard courses. Just like your undergraduate days in school, some courses are harder than others and will require more attention. Statistics is one of the courses that comes to mind—unless of course you're a math ~~geek~~, er, major. An important rule of thumb when planning your long-term course plan is that if you are planning on taking two or more courses in a given semester, you should always sign up for one difficult one and one easy one. As tempting as it might be to schedule two easy courses during a given term, it will most likely come back to haunt you at some point, when you will be stuck taking two difficult courses during the same term. That could prove to be your downfall.

If you are dreading the time when you have to take the statistics courses, set up your schedule so that you will take one stats class along with a class that you know will require less of you. It might even be one that is taught by a professor whom you've had before or who knows (and actually likes) your work. Better yet, this might be one of those times when you go for the independent study. However you go about it, pacing yourself is one strategy for the streetsmart graduate student.

Online courses: A virtual waste of time. We kind of just threw this section in here because it seems like it is becoming a trend in higher education. Not to be confused with the "Virtual University," many colleges are now offering online classes in lieu of traditional classroom courses. Generally you use a computer to get somewhere on the university's network, post bulletin board stuff, complete assignments, and meet with other students in chat rooms.

Most of our experiences with online classes have pretty much sucked. If your experiences are typical, you'll often get hung up with technical issues. If you don't get hung up with these things, you can almost be assured that one of your computer-illiterate-virtual-classmates will when you get stuck doing group work with him/her. Oftentimes these classes end up becoming more work than a normal class would require. The only reason we can see for putting up with this crap is if you absolutely have to take a course that can only be administered this way. What time you *think* you're saving in not having to drive to class is probably going to be wasted putting up with unnecessary bullshit and people who can't use computers. If you really are trying to learn something in grad school, don't bother with this shit until it's perfected. Over time, our views might change, but for right now, we don't put our stamp of approval on this unless you've done your homework and heard that a particular class is worth taking. In other words, be careful.

I need to drop your course. We feel pretty certain that you remember the drop add period from your undergraduate days. A tried and true strategy to consider using when setting up your semester schedule is known as the "I need to drop your course" strategy. One of our streetsmart colleagues used this brilliant system for setting up her course schedule each semester. Knowing that she was going to take two courses each semester, she instead always registered for three. She would then attend each class the first week of the semester to pick up a syllabus and determine how difficult each course would be. Then she would weigh the difficulties of each class and perform a careful balancing act—or, she would merely drop whichever class was the hardest. It was such an excellent system, it's kind of embarrassing that we didn't think of it first.

Weekly schedule. If you are a commuter, your weekly schedule is important. The drive itself can be a killer. For every minute you spend in class, you'll want to try to limit the number of minutes you're wasting behind the wheel of your car. Who wants to drive over to the campus three or four nights a week when skillful planning might cut it down to two or possibly even one night? We knew people who traveled to campus night after night looking more and more haggard as the semester wore on. This might be okay (even expected) if you're taking three classes at one time, but not for a simple course load of one or two classes.

During a traditional semester, class time needs to add up to approximately three hours per week (actual time varies for schools on quarters and/or schools that have Saturday classes). The university has the option of setting up class time in any configuration. They can create three one-hour classes, two ninety-minute classes, or one three-hour class. We recommend that, when setting up your schedule, you look for needed classes that are offered one night a week. If you must take classes that are split into two shorter periods, try to take two classes on each of those nights.

> *Relevant Story: An M.B.A. student we know took his courses in the "hard and fast" method. He took two classes per semester, finishing up his program in about a year and a half. As a commuter who lived more than an hour from campus, he found a way to minimize the time wasted in the car. After work on a particular night, he drove directly over to the campus to take two back-to-back classes. Each class lasted three-hours and he didn't get home until well past midnight. During this time period, the day (and night) of these classes and the following day were always pure hell for this part-time student with a full-time job—but for the rest of the week, he said it was worth it.*

CHAPTER 7

▼

Most people would sooner die than think; in fact, they do so.
—Bertrand Russell (1872–1970)

MANAGING YOUR CLASSES

Now that you have your long-term course plan and semester scheduling tactics pretty much under your belt, it's time to begin planning your strategies for managing your day-to-day classes. Sometimes, classes are pretty much the same as they were as an undergrad—read the material, listen to lectures, and take some stupid notes. Often though, the classes tend to be run a little differently. One difference between undergrad classes and graduate school classes is the size. Depending upon the level of class, the content, and/or the school you are actually attending, grad school classes tend to be capped at 10, 15, or 25 students. At the most, you'll probably see 30 students in a class. As a result, there tends to be a good amount of student-professor interaction that you didn't find in some of the larger undergrad classes.

Another difference you will find with these classes and the ones you left behind is the expectations. You are expected to acquire certain knowledge pertinent to your field, but the professors are really interested in seeing if you can *think*. Apply. Evaluate. Analyze. Connect. Synthesize. With that in mind, it should be noted that reflection, contemplation, deliberation, and consideration are often involved—as opposed to simple and boring rote memorization. The most irritating people are those who misunderstand, and seek to embarrass others with memorized facts (This is a good time to rent a copy of the movie *Good Will Hunting*. Pay particularly close attention to the bar scene.)

Humor vs. Serious Advice

Before we move on, the bottom line that you need to consider is this: be prepared for class by reading for comprehension and understanding—not memorization. How do the theories you're learning about in the classroom and the practicality of "the real world" in your field intermingle? What are some other ways of looking at the information? What is the *real* reason the professor is asking you to read this article?

Look, this ain't rocket science (unless you happen to be in a rocket science program—in which case you are more than welcome to ignore all of our advice related to stats classes and math geeks throughout this book). If you've been prepared for grad school through your undergrad studies and/or your career choice, the actual coursework within the classes should be (for the most part) a piece of cake. In other words, you should feel pretty competent inside the classroom. We suspect that this is where you need the least amount of tutoring. So rather than state the obvious in many places throughout this chapter, we'll just have a little fun...We recommend that, as you read through the following chapters of the book, that you are careful not to confuse the humorous parts with the serious ones. Both are sprinkled throughout the rest of the book. Though they are not overtly identified, we like to assume that our readers have (at least) half-a-brain and should be able to note the difference.

Regardless, the following sections will give you some pretty good ideas on how to make it through your classes without wasting too much time and energy. Since you're going to be involved in a lot of work, you might as well make it fun. With this in mind, be sure to note our suggestions for how you can have a little fun along the way. Our whole point here is that we want you to keep in mind that taking yourself or any of this stuff too seriously can be hazardous to your well-being and/or graduation.

Start every day off with a smile and get it over with.
—W.C. Fields (1880–1946)

Your First Day of Class: Sizing up the ~~Enemy~~, er, Competition

No matter how long you've been in graduate school, the first day of class is always interesting. Rather than let the first day be a source of additional stress, you can actually use it toward your own advantage. Make a special note of the people who talk too much before class starts. Are they nervous? Are they afraid of the course content? Are they know-it-alls? Did they try taking this course before and drop it because they were having a hard time understanding the content? These are the kinds of questions you are going to want to answer.

Depending upon your major and program of study, many grad school professors seem to use a grading system (regardless of how the "official" grading scale is published on the syllabus) in which the top students get A's, the bottom few students get C's, and everyone else gets B's. Although we don't have any empirical (big grad school word) research to back this up, it appeared to us that the students who were really nervous on the first day of class inevitably became the ones who got C's and/or dropped the course. In many courses, as long as you can perform better than these few people, you should be able to fairly easily pull off a B. So what, right? Well, we're telling you for a practical reason. It is important to realize that you should move as far away from these neurotics as possible, because you don't ever want to get stuck having to be their partners in class—they'll only hold you down.

Piggybackin'

The art of being able to work well with others is called cooperation. The art of being able to work well with others (while doing less work than them) is called "Piggybackin'." Let's face it. Some courses you'll take aren't going to be as important as others. The less important ones are ripe for piggybackin'.

Karl's Cheesy Beatles Analogy: Quick! Name the four Beatles. That's right, Ringo gets just as much credit (okay, almost as much credit) as John, Paul, and George—even though he never did jack and sucked at the drums. Ringo, you see, is the patron saint of piggybackin'. He wouldn't even have been a Beatle if Pete Best hadn't been scoring hotter chicks than Paul. Yet, he mastered the art of piggybackin' and never taking himself too seriously— resulting in him becoming one of the richest and most famous people in the world (not bad for a half-assed drummer who can't sing and has a big nose).

Okay, enough music history for now…The following sections should help you learn how to piggyback like a pro. Be warned, however, that you must use this strategy wisely and sparingly. If you piggyback too often and are too obvious about it, you'll quickly find that no one will want to work with you in the future. That could be a big problem down the road.

> *Pair up in threes.*
> —Yogi Berra

The GIG Approach: You too can be Ringo

The GIG Approach (yes, sports fans—coined here first!) is a teaching strategy that is utilized by many grad school professors. "GIG" simply stands for "Get In Groups." Professors seem to love this strategy, apparently because it frees them up from having to waste a lot of time planning and grading papers. A professor can easily turn a three-hour block of pure boredom into a "fun and exciting" class that gives his/her students lots of autonomy.

Oftentimes, the professor will tell the students to "get in groups" (GIG) to perform a task. Each group is usually expected to become the collective experts on a chapter from the textbook or one of the assigned journal articles (or some other crap). Once each group has met and become the "resident experts" on whatever the hell their topic is, they then have to teach it to the rest of the class. That's right! You're the teacher. Professors love this approach because it prevents them from having to do a lot of planning and grading papers. We don't blame them.

Sometimes, the professor will assign each group the task of actually finding all the necessary books and articles, creating a project, writing a paper and doing a class presentation. The professor will be sure to ask you to include a reference list so he/she can steal it from you (once again, we don't blame them for this, it is ingenious, really). Either way, group membership in a particular class can be a key determinant of your future grades. Maneuvering (or manipulating circumstances) for your own benefit is one of the concepts we're trying to get across to help you become streetsmart.

> *Hint: When groups are in the process of being created, be sure to choose the right group. If the professor uses some random technique to determine your*

group (e.g., he makes you count off), just ignore your number and join the group that seems the smartest or works the hardest. Somebody will inevitably come in late and the professor will simply tell him to join the smallest group. Never, ever willingly join the group with the nervous people mentioned earlier.

Working with a Partner

To become a true GIG Master, you need to learn how to piggyback effectively. Essentially, you want to work with overachievers and set it up so that you can do as little work as possible yourself—okay, maybe not as little as possible, but work that is as *painless* as possible. The key here is to be able to trust your group-mates, not necessarily to avoid work. If you suck at writing, don't do the writing part. If you suck at speaking in front of a group, don't do the presentation part. If you suck at art, don't do the artsy-fartsy shit. Neither of us generally minded speaking in front of a group, so we liked to use this to our advantage. We'd merely tell the other GIG members, "If you research, write and create this project, I'll present it to the class." Since most people seem to be afraid of public speaking, they usually jump all over this proposal.

Therefore, we would take on a minor role in the project, do little more than provide input while keeping track of our project's progress (and make suggestions for improvement) for most of the 15 week course, then we'd simply have to do one simple 15 minute presentation. Not only did we have to do very little work, but since we were the ones standing in front of the class presenting, we were in control of how our group was portrayed to the rest of the class and to the professor. This way, even if the actual project sucks, you can use your own knowledge and streetsmarts to salvage your grade. Unfortunately, before we perfected this technique, each of us was put in at least one bad situation.

> *Interesting Fred story: Early in my graduate school career, I got stuck in a group with some idiot who insisted on doing the group presentation. The rest of the group worked hard for weeks to put the project and presentation together. On the night of the presentation, our presenter screwed up so badly that it looked like we were all stupid and unprepared. Moral of the story: make sure you (or someone you trust) does the oral presentation.*

In addition to the control issue, another added bonus of being the group presenter is that it makes it look like you are the leader of the GIG group—do a good job and it's totally easy brownie points. With this in mind, though, we are not inferring that you should screw around without learning the material presented throughout your course. This method will backfire on you. Imagine standing in front of a class and trying to present something you know nothing about. You'll look like an idiot.

> *Helpful Hint: When piggybackin', don't work with the Dumbass, the Basket Case (for details, see chapter 9), or anyone who even remotely resembles these types. If you end up in a group with one of these people, by all means, don't let them do anything important...*

When and How to Take Breaks During Class

We're guessing that you're probably wondering why we are addressing breaks in a grad school guide. It's because breaks are sometimes the most important part of class. As a general rule, you should take two to three times as many breaks as are scheduled by the professor. Assuming your class is a three-hour block, we recommend taking breaks about 30 minutes before and after the professor's scheduled breaks. In addition to giving you a chance to use the facilities, it also reminds the professor that the class really isn't that interesting. Plus, it gives you an opportunity to buy food out of the vending machine. For some reason, eating during class always makes the time go by faster. A good break schedule goes something like this:

- BREAK #1 (30 minutes before scheduled break): Take a walk, go to the vending machine, say "hi" to important professors and then head back to class.

- BREAK #2 (scheduled break time): Piss out the Coke that you bought during break #1, hit on someone (if you're insecure and desperate like Karl) or call home and talk to your spouse (if you're whipped like Fred). Start up a conversation with one of the veteran students whom you've noticed seems to be "in the know." Finally, about a minute before the break is scheduled to end, begin talking with the professor about something interesting. This will lengthen the break (especially if you sense that he/she also has to take a leak), thus making you 15 new friends.

- BREAK #3 (30 minutes after scheduled break). This break is optional, but sometimes necessary to remove any remaining Coke you might have in your system and make a phone call if you need to. By this time you should pretty much know what time the professor will let you go for the day.

If you follow the strategy presented above, you can easily knock 45 minutes to an hour off of a class without much effort and missing a lot of content. This should increase your ability to pay attention for the rest of the class time, thus making you a better student (actually, that's bullshit, but it's a good excuse). Use your break(s) wisely.

> *Note: Some critics found this section offensive in the first edition—therefore we made sure to leave it in this one.*

Anybody who works is a fool. I don't work. I merely inflict myself on the public.
—Robert Morley

How Much Work Should I Not Do?

Tests, projects and papers are mandatory. All other work is optional. Well…it's not quite that simple, but we assume that you get the point.

> *Hint: If you've been paying any attention, you soon might begin to notice a pattern to the streetsmart guide as you read on. It deals mainly with the concept of planning ahead. You should always survey a graduate school situation **before** plowing head on into it. There are usually short-cuts available, you just gotta look for 'em. This isn't because you're a lazy ass—it's just that we believe your time is too valuable to waste on stuff that doesn't matter.*

Even if the syllabus says that you need to read articles X and Y for next week's, class, that doesn't mean you actually have to do it (see chapter 11 "The 3, er, 5 R's"). Sit back and take a closer look at the syllabus and determine *specifically* which assignments will determine your final grade. If an article will truly impact your grade, learn it inside and out. If, however, there is not an obvious connection, refer to the "toilet reading" section in chapter 11. Also, be forewarned, however, that some articles could be used to help you determine your area of interest and eventually the research topic in your dissertation, regardless of its lack-of-impact on a course grade. If that is so, then read it carefully, learn it and file it away.

Never mistake motion for action.
—Ernest Hemingway (1889–1961)

Classroom Discussions and How to Participate Effectively...

...Especially when you have not read the material thoroughly. As discussed in the previous section, numerous readings are always assigned for courses, but that does not mean you need to necessarily read them inside and out. Now, if an article or book is truly something you need to know for your dissertation, thesis or area of expertise, then that's a different story. If this is the case, then by all means read the damn thing, and read it thoroughly. It'll really come back to haunt you later if you don't. If, however, you are stuck taking some meaningless classes that have really nothing to do with your dissertation/thesis area, then avoid wasting time on unnecessary crap at all costs. If you are wise, you can become familiar with the material in the readings in other ways. This is the kind of thing that separates those who know how to *play the game* from those who don't. This section will introduce some effective strategies to try that will show everyone that you are on-the-ball even when you haven't exactly studied the stuff and gone through it with a fine-tooth-comb.

I wish people who have trouble communicating would just shut up.
—Tom Lehrer

Interrogation

In general, it's better to sound smart than to sound dumb (unless you're John Madden). Therefore, when it's your turn to talk, be sure to ask deep, conceptual questions and direct them towards other students who appear to have read the material. This will start an interesting, meaningful conversation while masking your laziness. Trust us, nobody else will know the difference.

If someone does call you on it, be extra humble and "admit" that you are "still waiting for the dust to settle while you process the information contained in the article." Make sure that you deflect any suspicion that you are a slacker. After all, you're "trying to not only make sense of the reading, but how it relates to some other bigger question." You should always talk in conceptual terms—the deeper, the better. This is an excellent way to redirect, sidetrack, and/or draw attention away from yourself and back to the content. In addition to this, it is always good to answer questions with deeper, conceptual questions. Vague bullshit worked for us, and vague bullshit can work for you.

If you sit in class and try to make conceptual connections between things you know and things you are learning, you'll be doing what you are there to do: Think and learn. By the time the class is over, you'll understand the content as well as (or better than) those who read it thoroughly. As you read the material, whether you are skimming it or going over it with a fine-tooth comb, try to see how the concepts fit into your overall conceptual framework of reality. Does it fit or is it contrary to your existing beliefs?

People who think they know everything are very irritating to those of us who do.
—Unknown

Ambiguousness

Ambiguousness. Is that even a real word? Anyway, never say "**I think**…blah blah blah…" No, no, no. All wrong. You should instead pick out some bigwig in your field—one that you understand well, or at the very least, one that nobody seems to truly understand—and say…"Isn't it possible that so and so…" or "Might so and so believe that blah blah blah…" Try to never sound like you already know the answer, because that always makes you sound arrogant. It also puts a little red target on your forehead. If you act like a know-it-all, everybody will be gunning for you and trying (probably successfully, too) to make you look stupid.

Never sound like a know-it-all…EVEN if your mind was made up before you set foot in the room…leave it open…or at least appear to, anyway. Generally, the more vague a word or concept is, the more powerful it is when utilized properly during class discussions (and dissertation defenses). Ambiguity is impossible to argue, just ask a politician. Once again, try to speak in conceptual terms, and never speak in absolutes (get it? *Never* speak in *absolutes!?*). [*hey—that was kind of hypocritical wasn't it.*]

I thoroughly disapprove of duels. If a man should challenge me, I would take him
kindly and forgivingly by the hand and lead him to a quiet place and kill him.
—Mark Twain (1835–1910)

Speaking of a Little Red Target

If you are the proactive type and you haven't read the material as well as you should have, or if you are fearful that the professor will call upon you out-of-the-blue to answer some specific question about the article, then begin looking for little red targets on your ~~enemies'~~, er, classmates' heads. Hey, sounds cruel, but they'd do it to you if they thought of it first. And yes, we know it's kind of geeky, but seriously, this can be fun. Okay, we wouldn't do this to someone we liked, but we wouldn't hesitate to do it to one of the Eggheads that are sure to be in the class. Consider this: You haven't read all of the material, but some smug, self-assured asshole is all, "blah blah blah, I know everything…This is the way it is…" That's your cue to listen to them carefully. Listen to the person and try to understand what they're saying. Who cares about the reading? That becomes secondary in this situation. Then, strike deadly when The Egghead makes the inevitable mistake.

How, you ask? Again, you'll need to think conceptually. Generally speaking, graduate school taught us to be careful when stating absolutes. "Always" is *always* a bad word. Few things "always" happen (except that "always" is *always* a bad word in grad school, get it?). Being sure of yourself is good, but it should be in a humble way. Listen for when someone is "absolutely 100 percent" certain that he/she is speaking "The Truth" when stating an opinion. Then strike fast. Who cares if you happen to agree with their "truthful" opinion. It's even better if you do. It makes you appear intelligent, knowledgeable, and simultaneously humble, while having the opposite effect on your unfortunate classmate. In this case you can preface your sarcastic lightening strike with, "even though I agree with you in theory, don't you think it's *possible* that…"

You state a one or two sentence question, then sit back and watch the person dig their grave deeper and deeper. As evil as this might sound, there is immense satisfaction in watching a Know-It-All sweat. Seeing this on paper leads us to feel an overwhelming need to apologize. Sorry, but it's true. Be sure to check out chapter 15 "The Joy of Intimidating Others" for more fun (*evil*) ideas.

> *It is better to be silent and be thought a fool*
> *than to open one's mouth and remove all doubt.*
> —Mark Twain

Silence Is Your Friend

Of course it is better to look smart than sound dumb. But if you don't know the material, then just shut the hell up and pretend to look interested (usually works). Or, bring lozenges to class and fake laryngitis (always works). Yup, that about sums it up. It worked for Mark Twain and it worked for us.

I Don't Know What the Hell is Going On

If called upon to answer some question that you are unable to answer, use one of the strategies in this section to avoid answering it. "I'm sorry, I haven't been following the conversation, I'm still stuck on [make up something about an issue that was debated earlier]…" This doesn't suggest that you're an idiot, instead it implies that you are a profound thinker who continues to ponder issues longer and deeper than the other people in the class.

> *Hint: If you are truly trying to learn throughout your grad school experience, then "getting stuck on a concept or new idea" ought to happen to you in classes where you have read the material and are trying to ponder issues that have rocked your world. If it doesn't happen, you're probably not trying hard enough.*

Try To Be the Last Person To Talk—NOT the First

This one is HUGE. When a particularly controversial or hot topic is being discussed, never say a word until all others are finished speaking. If you're lucky, the conversation will get so carried away, that you won't have to say a thing. Even more importantly, however, if it does come to a halt, get everyone's attention. Then pause for a moment (timing is everything), give a look of deep thought (slowly massaging your chin with one elbow on the table works great), and say something really provocative. The first people will say, "Wow, (s)he's really put a lot of thought into that" instead of "(S)he sure sounds like an idiot" (which is what they will be thinking about the know-it-alls). This strategy takes some practice, but when all is said and done, you'll look like frickin' Einstein (chances are, he had this technique mastered himself).

Hard work never killed anybody, but why take a chance?
—Charlie McCarthy (Edgar Bergen, 1903–1978)

How to Study

Although studying tends to suck, it is still possible to simply read the material and learn it reasonably well. Following is one such example.

Interesting Karl Story: I was taking a summer course that I particularly disliked (ok, it sucked some serious ass). Unfortunately for me, it was being taught by the head of the department (imagine that). In the middle of the four-week course, I had to miss two days to fly out of state to be the best man in a wedding. The trip forced me to miss the Thursday and Friday classes, but the course mid-term exam was to take place on the following Monday. No problem, I would just take my books with me and study. Unfortunately, the damn airline lost my luggage leaving me nothing to study (like she was ever going to believe that story—even though it was true). Fortunately, I had learned much earlier on in life that learning is much like playing a musical instrument or a sport: If I studied (or practiced) 30–45 minutes each day, I never had to cram for tests and still often knew the material better than my classmates. Although the airline had lost my book and notes, and I was not able to look anything over for four days prior to the test (that made up 40% of my grade), I still got an A on it. People who cram the night before don't learn anything, people who study a little each day do. Remember that proctologist we mentioned earlier?

When and How to Blow Off Class

There comes a time in every grad student's life when he/she simply has to blow off class. It is inevitable that other more important things will arise from time to time. When you run into this predicament, you might want to try some of the following strategies so that you can still learn the material and remain in good standing with your professor.

Know The Attendance Policy

Insecure professors often have an attendance policy. Take advantage of it. Use it (but don't abuse it) to your advantage. Why go to class unnecessarily? After all, you've got important stuff to do, right? Don't take this wrong, it's just that sometimes classes have little to do with the material you are responsible for knowing.

Interesting Karl Story: I took a religion class when I was an undergraduate student. Since it was a long class (a whopping hour and 15 minutes— which sucks when you have a hangover), the professor was kind enough to give us a break halfway through. His policy, however, was that he could take attendance at any point during class, therefore, if a student left class during break, he/she was marked absent for the day. Being the naïve dumb-ass that I was at that time, I sat in one of the front rows of the lecture hall. For some reason I had to leave class one day during break (probably to hurl). Sure enough, as luck would have it, the professor noticed that I had left, and therefore, decided to take attendance after the break. I was marked absent for the day and it hurt my grade. Had I had more streetsmarts at that point in my life, I would have known to sit in the back of the hall for any classes that have attendance policies like that.

Helpful Hint from Karl: It's a good idea to sit towards the front in courses that matter to your grade and/or dissertation.

*Helpful (amendment) Hint from Fred: Never, ever, no matter what Karl says, never, under **any** circumstance, should you **ever** sit in the front of a class. He's the token kiss-ass author in this book. This should serve as a reminder to you that everything you're reading in this book is opinion, and should be treated as such.*

Helpful (amendment) Hint to the Helpful (amendment) Hint to Fred From Karl: Screw you. I got higher grades than you, Dumbass.

Fred: Back 'atcha, Karl, I believe it was you who wrote, "In graduate school, grades don't matter. Once again, are you even reading the shit you're writing?

Karl: No. Why, should I be?

In the theater of confusion, knowing the location of the exits is what counts.
—Mason Cooley

Be Creative with Attendance

It is possible that two or more sections of a popular class (or one that is required by more than one department) are being offered on alternate nights. Make yourself aware of other sections of your class that your professor or others teach during the week. If you must miss a class on a particular night, for something more important (and what isn't more important?), and the professor is offering the same class on a different night, make arrangements to attend class on the alternate night instead.

*Helpful Hint: Making the effort to attend an alternate section of a class is likely to tell your professor two things: One, you are a very busy person, but two, you're a real "go getter." (Hint within a hint: You must be careful not to make the first statement without the second one. **Everyone** is busy. We observed many harried students who openly shared their personal problems with anyone within earshot. We also observed these same people who acted as though their professors were responsible for solving these personal problems. Though many of the professors are nice, caring individuals, they honestly couldn't give a rat's ass about how busy you are. If you can't handle the heat get out of the frickin' kitchen. They'll get annoyed with you, and they won't forget it. It's possible they'll even take it out on you during your comprehensive exams, your oral defenses or something like that). On the other hand, if they notice that you're busy but that you are still relaxed and taking care of business, you're probably in good shape.*

Helpful Hint (Part II): In this game, you want to begin earning their respect from day one. Then, later in the semester, if you are in danger of violating the attendance policy and you can't attend either class, your erratic attendance in both classes is likely to confuse the issue by the time the professor adds it all up at the end of the semester, anyway.

CHAPTER 8

▼

An alliance is like a chain. It is not made stronger by adding weak links to it.
—Walter Lippmann

NETWORKING: YOU SCRATCH MY BACK, AND I'LL SCRATCH YOURS...

Ask anyone who's been there. Graduate school is famous for being very political. This is the nature of the game, since professors and students alike need to expose their work to people in the right places. Whether you are seeking a letter of recommendation, a certain grade, or even trying to publish an important research study, it's all pretty much the same crap. You'll need to learn how to network (By the way, we both hate this kind of shit). The following sections will discuss different things to consider as you work to develop your networking plan. As with everything we seem to be mentioning, there are certain aspects of this that need to be understood before you proceed. We'll start with the simplest: With whom should you even bother trying to network?

With Whom Should You Even Bother?

Let's face it. Unless you're a politician, you can't be everybody's friend—and you don't want to be either. Make the right friends and you're set. Make the wrong ones and there's a rough road ahead. So who are the "right" ones? First of all, we're using the term "friend" loosely here. Friend is probably not even close to the right way to put it. Most of these people are not the type that you're gonna get excited about partying with. You should probably view these people as respected colleagues or associates more than friends.

Finding the Right People. Though we suggest that you try to be friendly enough with everybody, you'll look like an idiot if you try to be "agreeable" with all of them. In fact, it'll probably freak you out when you see how often (not to mention how seriously) people line up on different sides of the theoretical fence. Trust us, it can be war out there. You'll see it first in class discussions, then later in topical research interests and even in a person's chosen research methods. Academic types are funny. They tend to take their theoretical beliefs very seriously. As they do, they tend to take opposing views very personally. Be careful. If you attack their views, they may take it like you're attacking them personally.

Other Students. As you sit in class listening to others wax poetic about their beliefs, look for kindred spirits (yes, we recognize how dopey this sounds, just couldn't think of a better term for it). You're probably not going to find a clone of yourself, but their will likely be people who think similarly to you. These are the people you'll want to begin conversations with as you are waiting for class to start, during class breaks, and on your way out to the parking lot after class. We recommend that you share theoretical and practical insights with these people, and listen intently when they reciprocate. This is how you begin the process of networking.

As you talk more with these folks, you'll find that you click with some, while meshing with others like oil and water. Not to be mean or anything, but leave the negative ones by the wayside. Your job will be to become more friendly with those who seem like they're pretty cool (you'll soon realize that "cool" is a relative term).

> *Extra bonus hint: If you can swing it, these are the ones you'll want to gravitate towards in classes when the GIG approach (see chapter 7) is used.*

Find time to talk with them about experiences they've had, projects they are working on and anything else that might be of importance to your graduate school experience. Since their experiences have likely varied slightly from your own, you'll learn a lot of really good stuff. Offer them help when you can, and unwritten protocol says that they'll do the same for you.

Professors. You'll find a similar type of relationship can develop with your professors. Some of them are impossible. You'll probably notice the students who are on the other side of the theoretical fence from you always seem to have their noses stuck up these professors' asses. When you get trapped in a class with these assholes, we recommend that you simply get your work done then get the hell out. Don't waste your time trying to become overly friendly with them. They can't help you.

On the other hand, you'll find some pretty cool professors out there whose views and outlook on life are similar to your own. When you meet up with them, you'll want to get to know them in much the same way we describe above. At the very least, these professors are the ones you'll want to approach for the independent study. If you are a master's level student, you'll be wise to make sure your advisor is one of these types. If you are a doctoral student, make a list of these people. They're the ones you'll eventually want to get on your committee (More on this later).

Everybody Hates a Kiss-Ass

As mentioned earlier, nobody likes a frickin' kiss-ass. We do not recommend this approach. A kiss-ass is someone in a position that lacks power—in this case, the student—and who has his or her nose so far up the power broker's ass that you can see it come out of their mouth. Not only is ass-kissing sickening, but in most cases, it is counterproductive. Whereas professors are human and might like to have their ass kissed a little bit, they're not going to respect the "kisser." At the very least these ass-kissers get taken advantage of. At worst, nobody respects them. We believe that getting along with people is important, but never at the expense of losing respect. Of course everyone wants to be loved, but if we had to make a choice between love and respect, we'd rather have a colleague respect us than love us.

▼

CHAPTER 9

*Characters drop into whorehouses, have a little sex between paragraphs
and leave without advancing the plot.*
—Rhoda Koenig (Literary Critic)

THE OTHER STUDENTS YOU'LL MEET ALONG THE WAY

If you are easily offended, skip this chapter. If not, read on. A lot of the fun in graduate school lies in the people-watching. And with all of the different kinds of classmates you'll meet along the way, people-watching can be hilarious. You might develop a few close friends, but you will no doubt encounter a lot of freaks as well. You can either let these people get on your nerves and stress you out, or make the best of the situation and just have some fun. It's really up to you. We had a blast reminiscing when we came up with this chapter. The following sections will introduce you to a few of your future colleagues.

Note: This chapter is an equal opportunity offender. We use the pronouns "He" and "She" interchangeably throughout. Be sure to understand that each of these caricatures may hail from either gender.

When a book and a head collide and there is a hollow sound,
is it always from the book?
—Georg Christoph Lichtenberg (1742–1799)

The Dumbass

With all do respect, The Dumbass is a frickin' idiot. No one knows how the hell he got accepted into the program, but everybody knows he isn't getting out. Apparently The Dumbass is able to get accepted into the program by having good enough grades, a good enough entrance exam score, good enough looks, or is just extremely effective at bullshitting and kissing-ass. Other than that, however, this person really doesn't know jack about anything.

Although The Dumbass could probably make it through the coursework okay, this person will probably get busted during the oral exams or the prospectus defense. The Dumbass is generally good at cramming for a test, but never actually learns anything. As a result, this person generally has trouble passing the oral exam requirements. This is one of the reasons we do not advocate cramming for grad school tests. Although you might win the battle, you will not win the war.

One of the symptoms of an approaching nervous breakdown is the belief
that one's work is terribly important.
—Bertrand Russell (1872–1970)

The Harried Professional

Okay. Take your head and put it in your hands. Good. Now start rubbing your temples and forehead until they turn blotchy and red. For extra credit, use the tips of your thumbs to put extra pressure on your eyes until they swell and begin to appear puffy. Got it? Now take something wet and sticky and rub your hands through your hair. Is it sticking up yet? Good. Now you're ready to understand the Harried Professional.

This person is working in a full-time job that requires more time, dedication and responsibility than you will ever know. Trust us, you don't understand. This person also has a spouse and a couple dozen "high maintenance" children. Her pets and/or distant relatives are constantly sick, requiring their extra attention as well. She drives to campus eight nights a week through snow, uphill both ways...at least that's what she'd like you to believe.

In actuality, this person has responsibilities that are similar to yours. In fact, we suspect that she has fewer. Everything and everybody seems to "put her out" all of the time. Professors know her well, because most papers and projects are turned in late, usually accompanied by some wordy explanation. Stay away from this person. If you ever get stuck in a group with her, find a way to get the hell out. Save yourself!

Sanity and happiness are an impossible combination.
—Mark Twain

The Basket Case

The Basket Case is a person who realizes that he needs to get in and out of grad school to benefit their career. This person, however, has too much going on in his personal life to really do what it takes. Unlike the Harried Professional, this person really does have stuff going on. It's not like grad school is hard or anything, but there is a certain amount of tenacity required that the basket case just can't handle. As a result, he usually drops out after one or two classes. If this sounds vaguely familiar, then good—you've been paying attention. You read about one of these types earlier. You do not need to worry about The Basket Case...just don't waste your time trying to help him too much.

Foreign Students

After much debate we decided to take this section out—yet leave it in. This is very difficult to write about this without sounding racist and/or politically incorrect—two things you *never* want to do in graduate school. Stereotypes aside, numbers are pretty much the same in every language, whereas written and verbal skills are more difficult to translate. Just like English-speaking students, each individual has his or her own personality, work ethic, culture, and possible language barrier. Take this information into account when working with them on group projects.

The Person Who Hates Everything

Every once in a while you will meet somebody in graduate school who hates everything. The reason this person is even in graduate school is because she hates everything about society so much that she sees grad school as a sort of sanctuary.

She usually hides behind a theory called "critical theory." If that last sentence doesn't make any sense and/or isn't funny to you, read it after you've taken a few classes. It will begin to make sense then. Just remember, *critical theory*. Anyway, there really isn't anything to gain from the person who hates everything, but she's fun to watch. And we all know that comedy can be a good source of stress-relief.

Talk is cheap because supply exceeds demand.
—Unknown

The Know-it-All

During your first year of graduate school you'll certainly meet The Know-it-all. Although this sounds like a negative thing, it isn't necessarily so. The Know-it-all is generally just a person who has been in your program for a long time, and therefore knows a lot. You will be wowed (and maybe a little intimidated) at first by the Know-it-All, but it will wear off once you realize that he is not getting out of the program any time soon. We predict that you'll be sitting there in your cap and gown while he is still sitting in class.

We don't know a millionth of one percent about anything.
—Thomas Alva Edison

The Know-it-All (who knows nothing)

Similar to The Know-it-all is The Know-it-all-who knows nothing. This asshole is a lot like Cliff Clavin on *Cheers*. He's just a dorky guy who spits out trivial "facts" about shit all the time, and no one really cares enough to try to figure out whether or not he's talking out of his ass. It's really just not worth the effort. Once you realize that The Know-it-all is really The Know-it-all-who knows nothing, ignore this geek. Poking fun at him can be fun, too.

The Do-it-All

The Do-it-All is similar to The Know-it-all, but she is more behavioral in nature. Rather than just talking like they know everything, The Do-it-all actually tries to *do* everything imaginable in order to impress the important people. Although being the Do-it-all might earn you some brownie points, it 's really too much effort to be worth your while. The Do-it-all has no *streetsmarts* at all. If you happen to know a Do-it-all, give her a copy of this book. In case you didn't figure it out, The Do-it-All is *always* a good one to have in your group for group projects.

The King/Queen

The Do-it-all who has truly mastered the art of doing every possible thing required in graduate school (and beyond) is known as the King (or Queen if it's a woman, obviously). Not only is the King/Queen a combination of The Know-it-all and The Do-it-all, but this graduate assistant actually fools a lot of people into thinking that they are a real professor. The true King/Queen really needs to move on to a professorship at a major Research I university. If not, this person's entire graduate school experience was most likely a complete waste of time.

> *I like work; it fascinates me. I can sit and look at it for hours.*
> —Jerome K. Jerome (1859–1927)

The Lifer

The Lifer is someone who can confuse you at first. He might seem like a Know-it-All, a Do-it-All, or a King/Queen, but in actuality, he is none of the above. The Lifer is just someone who is in grad school forever with no apparent good reason. The Lifer is important, because he (like the basket case) makes grad school look really difficult to the rest of the world. In actuality, The Lifer is pretty much somebody who just doesn't want a job.

> *You've always made the mistake of being yourself.*
> —Eugene Ionesco

The Asshole

The Asshole is a self-assured, laid back student. The professors love this person even though he doesn't kiss their asses. It's all in the competence and the attitude. We recognize that it is very difficult to become The Asshole and still have people like you, but if you can do it, this is the ultimate goal in acquiring *streetsmarts* throughout grad school. The Asshole is not hated by everyone else—just someone who makes them envious. If you can do this, you should make not only a fine graduate student, but an excellent professor some day. If you truly work to master the concepts discussed throughout this book, you too, can become The Asshole. We wish you much luck, Grasshopper.

▼

CHAPTER 10

If you can't laugh at yourself, make fun of other people.
—Bobby Slayton

THE PROFESSORS YOU'LL MEET ALONG THE WAY

Sometimes, appearances can be deceiving. Although this chapter appears to be funny and blatantly irrelevant, it actually does serve a purpose (not to mention, it is one of the most popular with our critics). Just as we did with the freaky students in chapter 9 (Students You'll Meet Along the Way), we have documented the many characteristics of professors we met during graduate school and caricatured them for your "edutainment."

Concept Alert: Appearances can be deceiving. In other words, we urge you not to be fooled by the seemingly quirky behaviors your professors will display. Look at every aspect of the people you'll meet, and be careful when making judgments. Many of these people are not what they seem to be on the surface.

Parental Advisory: If you are easily offended skip this chapter also. It'll hurt your feelings.

This chapter is also an equal opportunity offender. We use the pronouns "He" and "She" interchangeably throughout this chapter. Be sure to understand that each of these caricatures may hail from either gender. Oh, yeah just one other thing. Have fun determining which professors in your department fit the following descriptions.

The Happy Hippy

Higher education is obviously called "higher" education for a reason. Okay, well maybe that's not really the case, but chances are that every college has a plethora (fancy grad school word) of professors who were hippies at one point in their lives. The male Hippy always has a beard and/or is going bald. Regardless, he may or may not have a ponytail. The female Hippy tends to have longer, unstyled, graying hair and wears long, rumpled hippy skirts and sandals.

Usually both male and female Happy Hippies are (still) into typical Hippy shit like Woodstock, The Grateful Dead, and "love-ins." They're (still) trying to save the world by hugging trees and going after seal clubbers. None of this is necessarily a bad thing. If you're not careful, however, some of these characteristics can interfere with your graduate school experience. It's important that you be on the lookout for them. Each of these professors tends to have a pet project or two that will require them to travel to a third-world country on a regular basis. Since these pet projects will be at the top of their priority lists, scheduling meetings could become a problem if you're not careful.

We recommend that you think about including The Happy Hippy on your dissertation/thesis committee. Usually they are good choices because they are all about ~~drugs, sex, and rock and roll~~, er, peace, love and happiness. Since The Happy Hippy naturally wants everyone to feel good about themselves, they are oftentimes willing to help with things that others might not. When working with these professors though, you might need to worry that they will lose your work in the frickin' rain forest, or worse yet, their office. They are notorious for forgetting meetings and losing track of time, too. Overall though, The Happy Hippy is usually a good person with whom to work. We recommend them "highly," but not necessarily as a major professor. Peace.

> *I've just learned about his illness. Let's hope it's nothing trivial.*
> —Variously ascribed

The Bitch

Obviously the term "bitch" (or bee-otch in some cases) is traditionally associated with females (except in prison). In this case, however, The Bitch professor might in fact be male. Do not necessarily assume that The Bitch in your department is a woman. The Bitch is someone who is a back-stabbing, kiss-ass. This person is working on the fast-track up the career ladder. The Bitch is an excellent manipulator who will use (and abuse) grad students and colleagues for everything they've got. When it suits this individual's purposes, The Bitch will chew up those whom they've used, spit them out, and throw them away. If it is more to their benefit, they'll just stab others in the back and laugh while the injured lay motionless in a pool of blood. Or worse yet, showing you how unimportant you are to them, they'll simply go right back to work.

If The Bitch recognizes you as a savvy grad student, it will be clear that you cannot be taken advantage of. Be aware that this person will still be ready to stomp you into the ground. The Bitch is someone who makes you think you have an "A" going deep into a class, then conveniently grades the final assignment subjectively so that you can be given a lower grade—just to prove who's in charge. If you recognize The Bitch in advance, try to avoid taking a class taught by him or her. If it is unavoidable, plan to get a "B" in The Bitch's class and don't bother worrying about it (you might still get an "A," just don't sweat about it). Be sure to steer well clear of The Bitch when choosing an advisor or your dissertation committee members.

> *One more thought about The Bitch: He/She is known for getting their feelings hurt if not asked to serve on your dissertation committee. When this happens The Bitch will target you for punishment down the road to get back at you.*

The Slob

Although usually very intelligent, The Slob is just that—a frickin' pig. Chances are you will never actually see The Slob's face, because there is so much shit piled to the ceiling all over the damn office that you can't even tell if "it's" in there. (We use the term "it," because it is often impossible to tell if the slob is male or female.) In addition to annoying grad students, The Slob also pisses off the other faculty members in the department. This is because once The Slob has messed up all it's own stuff so much so that it can't do any work, it then begins spreading it's disease all over the place. Under no circumstances do you want to work with The Slob any more that you absolutely have to. It will spill coffee on or lose your work, forget to attend meetings, and just waste your time. Stay away from The Slob at all costs. Oh, yeah, it often smells bad too.

The Professor's Professor (P.P.)

The Professor's Professor (P.P.) is the one member of the department who is highly respected by everyone (e.g., grad students, undergrad students, secretaries, the dean and other professors). The P.P. has published lots of important papers, is an excellent teacher, and has worked (or is working) her way through the tenure process honestly through lots of hard work. The P.P. earns about 50 cents an hour, because she puts in way too many hours of hard work for the paltry salary professors usually receive. The P.P. is someone who is very beneficial for you to work with. The P.P. will read your work carefully, give you excellent suggestions, and really teach you what you are supposed to learn in graduate school. If all professors were P.P.'s, we wouldn't have to write this book. If you can't read between the lines here, then maybe you shouldn't be in graduate school. Find this person and get her on your committee.

> *Sometimes a fool makes a good suggestion.*
> —Nicolas Boileau (1636–1711)

The Dummy

We've said it before, and we're sure we'll say it again. It doesn't take a genius to get a degree in higher education. Sometimes, somehow, some way, the Dumbass grad student detailed in chapter 9 finds a way to graduate. Needless to say, this person would be completely lost out in-the-field. This leads them back to…you guessed it, graduate school. Astonishing as it may seem, some other dumbass actually hires this person as a professor. Voila, you've got The Dummy. (We take the "ass" off at this point, because he now deserves a little respect.) You can identify The Dummy because you'll never be able to figure out what the hell he is talking about. The Dummy only learned three things in grad school and will reference those exact same three things repeatedly until he retires. Although you won't learn a damn thing from The Dummy, if you are a doctoral student, you might want one of them serve on your dissertation committee (see chapter 17 "Selecting Your Committee"). You will find this person to be very low maintenance. Dummies tend to lob softballs at you during your defense, and will likely want you to simplify your study's findings into tables and graphs—mainly because he's too frickin' stupid to actually understand your paper. Careful though, you don't want this person chairing your committee. That could be dangerous. If you want to create quality work, we recommend that you don't have more than one on your committee either. Enjoy The Dummy if you are lucky enough to have one in your department.

> *I may have my faults, but being wrong ain't one of them.*
> —Jimmy Hoffa (1913–1975)

The Ego

To sum up The Ego, "I'm right, and the rest of you might as well go home." The Ego is the professor whom you cannot, and should not even bother trying to argue with. This pompous ass loves to engage in higher order banter, but always with a nauseating air of condescension. The Ego thinks very highly of herself, and will go to great lengths to prove her self-worth. The Ego is the kind of person who feels better about herself when she is putting others down. The Ego never admits that she might be wrong, and God-forbid you (or anyone else) should disagree. For this reason, you should avoid this impossible personality at all costs.

Do not invite The Ego to join your committee or she will rip it to shreds, leaving you in the dust—that's assuming of course, that you can get her huge head through the door to begin with. The Ego will be happy to join your committee, but for all of the wrong reasons. She is in this game for only one reason: self promotion. Imagine for a moment that you've invited two or more Egos to join your committee…ugh…you can stop imagining now, the nightmare is over, or is it just beginning?

The Virgin

We were going to call this person The Newbie, The Rookie, or The Greenhorn, but we thought The Virgin would be so much more fun. The Virgin is someone who began her professorship career very recently. The Virgin is a follower. She piggybacks off other, more established professors, mainly because she hasn't learned the ropes yet. The Virgin often team-teaches classes and/or has a lot of guest speakers. Being The Virgin is not a bad thing by any means, you just want to make sure that you properly identify her. Although The Virgin won't necessarily be of much help to you, she (like the Dummy) can be a good person to include as a sort of "filler" on your dissertation committee. The only thing to be careful of, however, is that it's possible that The Virgin needs to do a lot of ass-kissing in her own right—thus, she may attempt to make you look bad if it will impress the right people. Include this person, but make sure you have the right kind of Virgin. As you might expect, you should enjoy this experience, but we recommend that you are careful, sensitive, gentle, and overall cautious with The Virgin.

The Guy No One Knows

Often times a department has a guy working there whom no one knows. You'll see his name on his office door, but never his face. He might even be dead. We don't know if this guy can really be of much help to you, but if we were betting men (and we are), we'd bet against it.

The "Cool" Guy

Chances are that you'll run into a professor who wants to look cool to his students. He comes into class, sits on his desk and says, "So, what's up?" We're guessing that The "Cool" guy was really a geek in his previously life, but he's got a second chance to be cool now through the professorship. Hey, maybe you'll even get lucky and The "Cool" Guy will make you feel important by letting you call him by his first name. Chances The "Cool" Guy can benefit you: better than 6 in 10.

> *There are some things that can beat smartness and foresight.*
> *Awkwardness and stupidity can.*
> —Mark Twain

> *A great many people think that polysyllables are a sign of intelligence.*
> —Barbara Walters

(The Egghead is so great, he gets TWO quotes!)

The Egghead

If you are sitting in class on the first day and your professor uses more than ten words you don't recognize within the first 30 minutes or so, run for the exit—this one's The Egghead. You'll recognize this freak from his smarmy attitude that screams, "I'm exceptionally bright and intelligent." If you don't recognize him by the attitude, just listen to him talk. He'll tell you the same thing, though you might not be able to understand what the hell he's even saying. "The indicator of this phenomenon is evident by taking a glimpse at how numerously abundant the student scholars are who apparently lack comprehension of the essence of this substance through which I am presently engaging in the process of edification." *Huh?* Let us translate. He's saying, "I'm smarter than you." Bottom line: For some reason, it makes certain people feel smarter when others are struggling to understand even the simplest of concepts.

This professor may be one who has been around for a while, but it's also possible that you'll find him in the Virgin category. This one will spend the next three months trying to make the easiest of concepts impossible to understand. The ridiculous thing about this ass-clown is that he is the one who doesn't understand...why his class evaluations always suck. Nobody (students *or* professors) actually likes (or respects) The Egghead because he acts self-important, when in fact he might actually be the lowest on the totem pole in the department.

Honestly though, after you've been in graduate school for awhile, this type isn't so tough to deal with. If it's one of your first classes though, it can be quite intimidating. You'll soon realize that this professor is a Know-it-all Who Knows Nothing (see chapter 9), but masks it behind rhetoric and jargon. If you hear about this person, we recommend that you avoid him. The benefits that you might reap are probably not worth the effort, although you might learn one or two new vocabulary words.

The Teacher

Generally speaking, the worst teaching in all levels of education takes place in college. Professors often see their jobs descriptions as merely doing research—the most important aspect in acquiring job security. Research helps professors work toward the almighty tenure. Teaching is often viewed as relatively minor side issue that interferes with their "real jobs." In some cases, professors might actually consider teaching important, but most of these people have no frickin' clue as to how to do it.

Every once in a while, however, you will run across a rare professor who is an excellent teacher. This person became a professor to teach others—not to conduct research. The Teacher will make time for you, explain things, give you direction and make your experience worthwhile. This is the best person to take a class with, and one of the best ones to have on your dissertation committee. Since there is only so much time in the day, this person has probably not done much publishing. As a result, The Teacher does not have much name recognition in the field.

The Teacher will, however, see to it that you learn what you're supposed to learn in order to get through the program. She will help you put together a good committee and let you put your name on some of her research, (see chapter 17 "Selecting Your Committee") take meaningful courses (see chapter 6 "Nobody Cares About Your Degree"), and go over and above what is called for in order to help you. Identify The Teacher early on in your program and work with them before they get their ass kicked out for not making tenure. The Teacher makes a great major professor—if they don't get canned too soon.

Summary

At first glance this chapter might look like it was designed simply to insult graduate school professors. If that is what you are thinking, please look at it again—more closely this time. Identifying the personalities of the various professors in your department will help you assemble a much more functional dissertation committee when the time is right. The importance of this can NOT be understated! Although some of the personalities are a bit overstated for amusement purposes, we suspect that you'll find some professors in your department who'll look almost exactly like and behave as if they came right out of this chapter. More of them, however, will look like a combination of two or more caricatures. Once again we urge you to read between the lines and look for the concepts presented throughout this chapter. When assembling your committee seek professors who have your best interest at heart. These professors are those who have both the time and inclination to help you succeed. We've also recommended that you look for professors who are competent, not only with a strong knowledge base, but also with the experience and ability that will help you get things done.

BEWARE—Certain combinations of professors' personalities can be hazardous to your graduation!

CHAPTER 11

▼

THE 3, ER, 5 R'S

Back on the prairie in the one room schoolhouse, Laura Ingalls and her "good friend" Nellie Olsen were only required to learn 3 R's. Of course, Laura was just trying to get through the fourth grade so she could become the all-knowing teacher and "learn" her students better. And Nellie…well, what was up with that bitch, anyway? In the olden days, the 3 R's were more than enough for farmers and factory workers. In order to earn an advanced degree in this day and age, however, students are required to go far beyond those three basics. The way we figure it, there are actually five "R's" associated with modern graduate school:

1. Readin',

2. wRitin',

3. 'Rithmetic,

4. Researchin' and

5. Regurgitatin'.

This chapter is designed to provide you with some solid pointers on how to handle each of these important areas. The better you can handle the "5 R's," the more successful you will be in utilizing your valuable time while "Getting Through" graduate school. Unsaid but inferred, handling these issues effectively will make it more likely that you will be able to move forward into the "Getting the Hell Out" phase—and by moving into that phase, we're not talking about quitting.

> *I've given up reading books. I find it takes my mind off myself.*
> —Oscar Levant (1906–1972)

Readin'

Think back to a time in high school or college when you were reading a boring-ass textbook. Attempting to concentrate, your eyes move across and down each page time and again, your hands turn the pages slowly as you "finish" each one…an hour or so later, you get to the end of the reading, only to realize that you weren't actually reading squat. In fact, your glazed-over eyes were simply moving back and forth across the page in a fog. In other words, you didn't actually absorb any of it. Sound familiar?

By-and-large, the most time-consuming part of grad school coursework is the reading. In just about every course you will take, the professor will require you to read something for *every* class meeting. Sometimes it'll only be a little, and most of the time it will be relatively reasonable (think in hours, not minutes). In some cases, however, the amount of reading can be ridiculous—abbreviated summer courses or "mini-mester" classes are notorious for this. The good news is, you've chosen an area you are interested in, right? The bad news, though, is that most academic types don't write to entertain their readers. Most grad school readings are "thick" in content. Know what we mean? Yup, reading academic journals can be a lot like trying to swim through molasses. You can do it, it's just slow and often agonizing.

If you can get a solid handle on the reading part of grad school, you'll be in good shape. A "solid handle," means that you understand the most important material without wasting too much time with the less important stuff. When you see the sheer amount of reading, you'll appreciate why you want to cut down on the time. When it is time for comprehensive exams, you'll grasp why comprehension is so important. The following sections discuss ways to cut your reading time down to a bare-ass minimum—most importantly, *while still* **comprehending** *the material.*

I took a course in speed reading and was able to read War and Peace in twenty minutes. It's about Russia.
—Woody Allen

Toilet Reading

One of the best methods we've discovered to help with the ubiquitous (awesome grad school word) task of drudging through boring readings is called "Toilet Reading." It's not ground-breaking, we know—people have been reading magazines while taking a dump for centuries. What does make our approach innovative, however, is the use of a highlighter. Be sure to keep quality highlighting markers in easy-to-reach places near the toilet paper rolls in every bathroom of your house. Toilet reading is especially effective for short to medium length journal articles. They aren't too heavy in terms of content or weight and can be easily managed with one hand. These are usually the articles that will be discussed during class, so you'll look like a real go-getter when you show up to class and the professor can see evidence that you obviously read the shit (pun intended).

Remembering that many of our suggestions are coaching you in terms of abstract concepts and not simple "literal" meanings, this suggestion is intended to remind you to use your time wisely. Oh, don't get us wrong. We *are* literally suggesting that you use the bathroom for reading. But the bathroom is not the only place where you can gain a little solitude, and it isn't likely the only place you can get things done (if it is…we need to talk). We suggest you reflect upon your life and think creatively. You might get the same thing done on a bus, a time-consuming subway ride, at your child's protracted baseball practice, at a mind-numbing meeting, during lackluster sex, or any number of other places.

Note: In case you haven't figured it out yet, this book itself is designed specifically for "toilet reading."

Where do I find the time for not reading so many books?
—Karl Kraus (1874–1936)

How to Not Read Boring Material

Let's face it, a lot of grad school reading wasn't really intended to be all that interesting—actually none of it was. Like The Egghead Professor (see chapter 10), many researchers seem to have the idea that they should deliberately make their articles difficult to understand. Difficult to understand translates into, "takes longer to read." They do this so that readers will be awed by how smart they sound and maybe mistake it for quality research. Sometimes we think some material is written in difficult language in order to intimidate readers into believing whatever bullshit the author concludes.

Anyway, when you are required to read a boring quantitative study (one with heavy statistics), just go right ahead and read the final summary *first*. The summary should tell you the basics of what was discovered during this study and why it matters. Next, go back and read the introduction and methodology. This will tell you the reason why the researcher thought his study was important, and how the research was actually conducted. While you are reading, be sure to highlight all the important sentences in the summary, the intro, and the methodology.

Only after you've thoroughly read the summary *first*, should you even consider going back to the intro. You should then go through most of the rest of the article by simply reading the first and last sentence of each paragraph. If something seems worthwhile or simply catches your eye, by all means read that too. Just don't waste your time reading everything if you don't need to.

The Icing and the Cake

Although the previous system should work effectively for much of the hot air you have to read, there are two notable exceptions to the rule.

1. If certain readings have been identified as crucial to your area of interest or concentration, you need to learn them inside and out. Period. Every field has its "fathers" and "mothers" (e.g., Freud—"father of psychoanalysis", Einstein—"father of quantum physics", Heffner—"father of mainstream smut"). If your professors seem to continually refer to certain researchers, books and articles, get to know them as well as you can. Try not to take shortcuts, because you'll likely get called on it at some point. This is the kind of shit (pun intended) that the proctologist mentioned previously skimmed over when he shouldn't have. Consider these readings to be "the cake," and the toilet reading crap as "the icing." (Yum.)

2. If a professor in your department has written a book or published some "important" research in a journal, you can bet your ass that he/she will make you read it. If you are required to read something *written by the professor* who is teaching your class, then you're pretty much screwed in terms of shortcuts. Unless, he had a grad assistant write it for him, he

probably should know the piece inside and out. This means that he can also tell if you have actually read it and understand it. Sometimes, you just have to punt. Our advice is to just read the damn thing and act like it's important. This is, however, a great opportunity to ask some insightful questions during class about the professor's work. If you don't come across as too much of a kiss-ass, you'll probably earn some brownie points. If you are asked to write a response to it, then make it sound important.

Our American professors like their literature clear, cold, pure and very dead.
—Sinclair Lewis (1885–1951)

wRitin'

We hope you don't mind writing, because that's what graduate school is all about. Sure, you can read, but can you write? The following two sections are intended to help you become a better grad school writer. We've separated them into two distinct categories, WRITING skills and, uh, writing SKILLS. If you've gotten into graduate school, you're probably at least a serviceable writer, but in grad school, there is more to the game. The first part deals with the actual process of writing (which we assume you can already do), while the second part deals with related skills and strategies that might help you do the first part better at your university. That's the *Streetsmart* Section, it's probably the most important part. You'll see what we mean…

WRITING Skills

As stated above, we already assume you can put a sentence together, so this section is fairly short. As always, though, there are a couple of concepts that we recommend you follow.

Using Big Words…and actually knowing what the hell they mean. Have you ever been watching a television interview and noticed an athlete, musician or actor using big words inappropriately while trying to sound intelligent? What effect did this have on your opinion of them? If you're like most, then you probably rolled your eyes, shook your head and thought to yourself "it's a damn good thing this idiot can play a sport or an instrument, because he sounds like a frickin' idiot."

How then, does this relate to your writing? The authors of this book are strong believers in writing for the simple purpose of eloquently communicating your thoughts in a manner that is easily understood by the intended audience. Now, re-read that last sentence. Understand what we're trying to say? Good. Did you have to read it more than twice for comprehension? Then it's a bad sentence.

> *Dumbass Story: When asked why an article that a professor wrote was so difficult to read, he replied, "It should be—it was difficult to write."*

Although you need to sound like an expert in your field (unlike us at the moment), it's probably best to present your written ideas in such a way so that people can understand them easily. The point of scholarly writing is to tell others in your field about the important things you've learned—not to impress them with big-ass words. Keep your writing simple, clear, and *to the point*! Do not try to impress people like the Egghead and Know-it-All's (see chapters 9 and 10). It's easy to get caught up in all the jargon and research terminology when you write, because everybody else does, but we suggest that you avoid falling too deeply into that trap. When you need to use jargon and professional terminology, do so, and then get the hell away from it and back to something that sounds like you are having a professional conversation with a colleague—not too stuffy, but not too folksy either.

If you didn't already know that we believed this from the way this book is written, then you've really got your work cut out for you. Bottom line, you're not a frickin' thesaurus. If you're smart, you will learn how to use the one on your word processor. When you do, though, keep this in mind: Use big words sparingly, and when you do, use them effectively.

No matter what graduate school program in which you are enrolled, you're gonna do a lot of writing. That's the nature of graduate school. Though many people suffer mentally every time they sit down at the computer, writing really shouldn't be that difficult. If you can communicate your thoughts when you talk, then you should be able to communicate them just as easily in writing. There is a simple strategy for making this work. Don't try to write over your head. This will cause two problems: One, attempting to use words you are unfamiliar with is akin to literally trying to translate your thoughts into a "foreign" language. This often results in unnecessary mistakes and "writer's block"—since your thoughts will not flow out of your brain and on to your paper easily. Two, after you "suffer" through many long nights of translation, your paper is going to suck—bad. It will end up sounding like The Egghead professor we mentioned earlier. Maybe worse, you could sound like the dumb jock/actor/musician.

Bottom line: If you can't easily communicate your thoughts to another human through your writing (no matter how many big words you are using), then you're not doing a good job. Don't be a frickin' Egghead.

Writing, reading and editing. You may have never thought about this, but parts of your writing probably don't "read" the way you intend (Fred's almost never do). Professors will always point that out—it's their job to help you become a better writer. If that hurts your feelings, you need to grow some thicker skin. When you are the author of a piece of writing, it's almost impossible to see your work objectively. During self-editing, you will certainly find typos and other obvious transgressions. Unfortunately for you, though, some of the more subtle mistakes remain. When you are proof-reading your own writing, you're probably reading what you *want* your paper to say, not what it actually says.

Hint #1: The best method for limiting these types of mistakes is to ask someone else to read your papers, and edit accordingly. If you do not have someone you trust to read your papers thoroughly, we recommend printing a hard copy of everything you write and read it out loud to yourself. You will find that a lot of things that made sense in your head didn't necessarily come across that way to the reader.

We've noticed that when we write, the general content is usually pretty good after the first rough draft, but there are always things that can stand improvement (even at the time of publication). Some ideas may have been explained in a confusing or unclear way. Maybe the paper has been organized in a way that doesn't do the topic justice. Sometimes a paper assumes readers know more than they do. In other words, the writer might need to add more background. Other times, ideas might come across as condescending. An author might have added too much background and insulted the reader. Still other times, unexplained jargon might be used. Reading your own paper 50 or even 100 times isn't likely to reveal all of its flaws.

Hint #2: Remember who your audience is, and write for that audience.

Topic sentences and all that kind of crap. We may be oversimplifying this just a bit, but what the hell. Scholarly writing is basically a formula. Topic sentence, then explanation of that topic sentence. Simple concept. Be sure to use clear and concise topic sentences throughout so that people who skim your work will still get the gist of it. Realistically, professors have shit-loads of reading to do every day, and they won't always be able to spend the same amount of time reading the crap you turn in as they do reading the work of some more important Big Wig's. Simply make sure your introduction is clear and to the point, your conclusion is clear and to the point, and that you have clear topic sentences throughout the rest in case your professor only has time to skim over your work.

> *Bonus: Think back to the "Readin'" section...keep this same concept in mind when you are running low on time!*

Repetition, reiteration, replication, duplication, etc. Since some ideas are particularly important in your writing, you might need to repeat them clearly in your conclusion in case a reader chooses to only read that one section of your piece. If you don't do it, and she skims it, then she might criticize you for missing something important. On the other hand, if you follow this advice and she reads the entire piece thoroughly, she might criticize you for being repetitious. Either way you're likely to hear some criticism about the way you handle this problem, but we still feel it's better to err on the side of conservatism (well, in some cases), and be criticized more for trying to get your point across rather than not making it clear enough.

Every paper needs to have a colon in the title. They just do. No one seems to know (or even ask) why, it's just what grad school people do. We know, you're thinking, "Thanks for the valuable info." Hey, at least it's a start.

Writing SKILLS

The grammatical aspects of writing aside, we assume that you expect to become a better writer from all the practice you'll get while attending graduate school. Seriously, you're going to get a lot of practice, so there are some things you'll need to know (and some skills you'll probably want to have) if you want to be efficient. In addition, there are some politics that come into play as your professors assess your work. Yes, they will assess your work. If you think you're a "writing god" when you enter, you're gonna get knocked down a peg or two immediately. In fact, you're gonna get your ass knocked right off your wobbly little pedestal. In order to avoid this (and to keep your ego from getting too bruised), we will share some time-tested *streetsmart* methods that will help you to deal with the inevitable critique. Finally, this section will lead you to the holy grail of grad school writing: How to become an expert on a topic while saving yourself years of time and thousands of dollars.

To Type or Not to Type: That is the Question. As always, we start with the obvious. Well not really, but it is worth addressing. Basically, they are two types of people in the world: typists and non-typists (sometimes referred to as "hunt and peckers"). In our opinion, computers have really helped to champion higher education. If it weren't for word processors, we would have never wasted our valuable time writing this damn book. The ability to type 75 words a minute doesn't hurt either. If you are a typist, you have it made. You can blow through papers quickly. If you are a pecker, you will probably take forever to get things done and/or have to waste money paying someone else to do it for you. Knowing how to use the advanced tools (e.g., formatting, tables, spell-check) on your word processor is a real plus, too.

Although it might be too late for you to learn how to type, you can at least pass this information on to others. Some people seem to still have the idea that "if you're going to amount to anything in this world, you'll have someone to do the typing for you." Bullshit. Whereas, that might have been true in the dark ages, it can be a huge pain in the ass in grad school today. With the advent of word processing, it's really not all that hard. *Moral of the story: Don't be a pecker.*

Wasting money to save money. Although both authors of this book are accomplished typists (whatever that means), there were times when we found it was to our advantage to have a true "speed typist" type things for us. Rather than spending two years typing transcripts from audio-taped interviews and focus groups when we wrote our dissertations, we each paid a professional to do it for us. She was experienced, relatively inexpensive, fast, and 100% accurate. We'd merely conduct a 20 to 30 minute interview, give her the cassette tape, and the next day she'd bring back the transcripts perfectly transcribed and formatted. With the transcripts in hand, we simply had to copy and paste the stuff we wanted to use from the interviews into our dissertation text and we were on our way—countless hours of interviews perfectly transcribed for around 300 bucks. This enabled us to spend our time concentrating upon the important conceptual aspects of our studies, which ultimately lead to an earlier graduation date. Our early graduation allowed us to begin enjoying the benefits of our doctorates immediately.

Helpful Hint: A lot of times it is okay to "waste" money in grad school.

A.P.A., M.L.A., (and/or other ~~useless~~, er, required paper formats). In your first graduate school class, find out what format your school expects you to use when writing papers. How wide are the margins? Which fonts are acceptable? How do you format references within the paper? How do you list them at the end? Do you put one space or two after the end of a sentence? When should you use a colon as opposed to a semi-colon? We could go on for days here, but you get the idea, right?

In our programs, we used the A.P.A. (American Psychological Association) format. No, this does not mean that we're a couple of shrinks (we're not). Though some schools have their own format and there are others out there, A.P.A. format is simply one of the most common standardized formats used by researchers in higher education. It doesn't really matter which set of guidelines you will be required to use. Whatever it is, it'll suck. Just start using the format immediately. Some professors will be really particular about how it is done, while others will appear not to have a clue. The only way to get comfortable with a format is to practice using it. Start practicing it early in your program, use it consistently, and you won't have to worry (too much) about it later.

It is salutary to train oneself to be no more affected by censure than by praise.
—W. Somerset Maugham

If you are not criticized, you may not be doing much.
—Donald H. Rumsfeld (1932—), Secretary of Defense

[*another concept so important that it gets two quotes!—although one is meant to be more humorous than the other…*]

They're Going to Tear it Apart Anyway (Get Over It)

Though you are sure to hear your share of compliments during the next few years, the overriding question we have to ask you is, how well do you handle criticism? Let that one sink in for a few seconds…then read on. When you write, do you get emotionally attached to your words as soon as they appear in print? Do you get annoyed or hurt feelings when someone points out that something you wrote kind of sucks? In other words, can a friend, a colleague or a teacher critique your writing without you becoming defensive? Can a spouse give you suggestions on your writing without tears springing from your eyes? Our advice: Grow thicker skin, or just completely forget about graduate school. Drop out, quit, withdraw, give up. Get a frickin' puppy. We don't care, just do something else, or you'll spend the next few years in a shitty mood.

Throw Me a Frickin' Bone Here

Any time a paper is read by a professor, they're gonna rip it apart. They might do it in a nice way, or they might leave teeth marks on it. Who knows? Either way, professors tend not to feel like they are doing their job unless they offer you some sort of criticism (worthwhile or not). That's why, when they offer you the chance to turn in an initial rough draft for criticism before submitting the final paper, just do it—and expect to be critiqued.

You see, a rough draft is exactly that. A *rough* draft. In other words, don't put all of your blood, sweat, tears, and emotional investment into something that you feel is a final draft quality. Otherwise, you'll get discouraged when you get it back. Don't get us wrong, you've got to produce something with merit. Just put your thoughts on paper in a clear and concise way. Use proper grammar and try to sound like you can put a sentence together and that you give half a shit. Try to make sense. And by all means, use spell check. Don't waste your professor's time by giving them a paper that looks like you wiped your ass with it. Then, of course be sure to include ALL of their suggestions in the final draft.

Always Turn in a "B"

Always Turn in a "B". Well, that's probably taking it a little to far, but you might find this technique useful for certain occasions. It's this simple—just turn in a "B" paper when given the opportunity for revision later. We recommend leaving some easy-to-fix, obvious holes in your paper. Trust us, they're going to criticize your paper no matter what you do. Like a savvy politician, draw their attention to something that is clearly fixable. We suggest that you choose a certain issue not to spend your time on during the initial edit. Something that you can see is a little sub-par, but not necessarily something that is essential to the overall meaning of the paper. Leave it a bit rough, saving the polish for the final edit. We recommend that you leave the issue you are most unclear about as the unfinished one. That way you can get the professor's feedback while making him feel as if he is earning his paycheck. When you write the final paper, address all of his corrections clearly, and you won't feel like you've been hit over the head with a mallet, Everyone is happy.

> *To reiterate our earlier message: Try to understand what we're saying, and don't take it out of context. While turning in a "B" paper is advisable, turning in a piece of shit at **any** point is counterproductive.*

> *Everywhere I go I'm asked if I think the university stifles writers.*
> *My opinion is that they don't stifle enough of them.*
> —Flanner O'Connor (1925–1964)

Less is More

Ever heard the phrase, "Jack of all trades, master of none"? If you learn nothing else from this book, learn this: **Become an expert on one topic and try your very best to hand in papers on the SAME damn topic for EVERY course**. This is not always possible, but you can come pretty close. This is the reason that you want to narrow down a dissertation/thesis topic (your "topic of interest") as early as possible. Once you have your topic, begin writing the first draft of your literature review immediately (more on this in Chapter 20 "Your Dissertation/ Thesis"). In other words, don't be a Jack [ass].

We speak in absolutes here, but this does not mean that we advocate doing anything unethical. Just be smart. You can't just print out an old paper for a new class. You get caught doing that and you'll deserve what you're gonna get, which is booted out of school and sent to grad school jail. You should pick a topic you are interested in, then investigate different aspects of this topic throughout your school career. When you write about your topic, you will simply be adding to and tweaking ideas from papers you have previously written. This will allow you to build up your area of interest over time and get feedback from a variety of professors along the way. Adding new ideas and references to each "new" paper you turn in will eventually save you a huge headache when it becomes "chapter 2" of your dissertation/thesis (more on this in chapter 20).

In addition, as it gets better, it will make your professors realize how much you are growing as a writer. If you are in a doctoral program, your "improvement" will go a long way in determining how many more classes you need to take before your committee has determined you are ready for the "Getting the Hell Out" phase. If they believe that you've gotten to be an expert on something and have become a proficient writer, then they'll be ready to help you move on to the next step.

> *Helpful Karl Story: I was fortunate enough to put my dissertation commit-*
> *tee together very early in my program of study (see chapter 17, "Selecting*
> *Your Committee"). I met with my major professor and gave her a list of the*
> *professors I was considering asking to serve. She crossed out the shitty ones,*
> *and told me to talk to the ones whose names remained on the list. While*

asking each one to serve on my committee, I presented him/her with five potential research questions around which I considered basing my dissertation study. By the time I had met with all five professors, they pretty much all liked the same topic. Therefore, that became the focus of my dissertation and most of the paper(s) I wrote from that day on in grad school. By the time my coursework was finished, so was chapter 2 of my dissertation.

Write All Paper(s) the First Month of Class

Here's the bottom line: procrastinators suck at the grad school game. There's no way around it. If you're a procrastinator, you're going to struggle. Think of it this way: if you have a paper to write that you think will take three weeks, it's gonna take three weeks whether your write it towards the beginning of the course or the end. As soon as you get a feel for what a course is going to be about, start working on your final paper. If you do this you will find that the books and articles you need have NOT yet been checked out from the library, you will end up with a much better paper at the end, and you will experience a lot less stress. Best case scenario: You finish your paper before the course is half finished and get to screw around the last half. Worst-case scenario: When the course is half finished you realize that your paper was not going in the right direction. If this happens to you, then you still have plenty of time to change it (we recommend, however, that you save the first paper, 'cause you might be able to use parts of it in a different class). It's really not that hard. You'll still be finished before everybody else and have a better paper to show for it. Procrastinate, and you'll end up a basket case (see chapter 9).

Writing Quality Papers: Why the Internet is (Not Necessarily) Your Friend

When checking out the title of this book, shallow people are likely to assume that we are advocates of cheating and plagiarism. You know what they say about people who assume, don't you? As we've mentioned throughout, however, we do not support any type of dishonesty. By the time students get through college, they've probably discovered a number of websites that offer free (or almost free) term papers to download. Whereas, it is possible to get away with this, we believe that in graduate school you need to come away knowing something.

The fact is that a lot of universities are getting wise to this sort of thing and are beginning to look out for it. They obviously can't read every paper on the Internet to determine whether or not yours is original, it's pretty easy to figure out that you're talking out of your ass when you have to present your paper or defend it to a small group of people. Don't buy or steal other people's work unless you're an idiot and are willing to get your ass kicked out of school for doing it. If that doesn't worry you then go for it, Dumbass. But don't blame us—we're not in your corner.

Choose Interesting Topics.

A much better alternative to plagiarism is to actually choose a topic based on something that really interests you. No, we're not being sarcastic. Really. This advice sounds totally lame, but you'd be surprised how many boring, stupid, insignificant topics people choose for their dissertations (e.g., *Perceptions of Elementary School Principals Regarding the Floor Covering's Function in the School's Physical Environment and a Comparison of Elementary School Students' Performance with Sound Intensity Levels in the Classroom*). Yes, that's real.

The fact is that if you're going to be stuck writing and thinking about this damn thing for a couple years, you might as well find it sort of interesting. You'd be surprised at how you might be able to turn something that interests you into a dissertation topic. For example, an ethnomusicologist (once again, yes, that is a real major) actually wrote his dissertation on a rock group. It's called, *Grand Designs: A Musical, Social and Ethnographic Study of Rush* (Check out this website if you don't believe us. He's Karl's hero: http://www.students.yorku.ca/~mcdonald/). On a side issue, note the colon in the title. As mentioned previously, no graduate school paper is complete without one.

Saving Time and Money...Again

Some universities will actually offer a class on writing your dissertation/thesis lit review. If you really think you need the help, take it. On the other hand, if you've learned the most important thing from this book, don't. While all the other students in our department were taking an extra 15-week course to help them write their literature reviews (basically a support group for losers), ours were already finished. The literature review class seems to only be good if you are a real procrastinator who can't accomplish anything unless you have someone telling you to do it constantly. If this is you, have fun taking that class. If you are like us, however, enjoy the hours of extra free time, take the hundreds of dollars you'll save, and throw a party in your honor.

Don't be Sorry. Be safe.

Computers are beautiful. We couldn't have (or maybe simply wouldn't have) made it through grad school if it wasn't for computerized word processors. Our advice: Back everything up in at least TWO places, and then email it to yourself! We can't even begin to explain the importance of this! When we were in the process of writing important documents (e.g., dissertations, this book) we saved them on our hard drive, a floppy disk, and Zip disk, and often emailed copies of it to ourselves and our families—just in case!

> *Interesting Karl story: There was an incident that took place at the university where my mom attended undergraduate school. During the 1960's when people were boycotting the Vietnam War, the students in town started rioting and lighting things on fire. The oldest building on campus was burned to the ground during the riot. My mom's transcripts and graduation information—along with a lot of important research documents— were stored there. This was in the days before personal computers, so these would have been documents that were hand-written and typed on a typewriter. Oops.*

Although we no longer have to save everything solely as a hard copy, shit still happens. We have viruses that wipe out computers, floppy disks that get broken, files that can be easily plagiarized, and a bunch of other crap they didn't have to deal with in the 60's and earlier. Essentially, back all of your shit up early and often. Just make sure you keep track of the names and location(s) of your most recently updated files. The more places and the more often you save your work, the more out-of-date files you'll end up having to sift through to find your most recent document. When all you want to do is work, the search can be maddening (Fred is notorious for this...I can't even begin to tell you how many times he's screwed this file up. What a tool).

One other thing to consider—if you have the ability to swing it, try writing and saving your work on a computer that you do not use for anything else. Karl keeps two computers that he uses regularly—one for doing serious work (unlike this), and one for doing all the other stuff. If you use the same computer for writing your dissertation that you use for downloading illegal mp3 files and movies, you're asking for trouble. Consider yourself warned.

'Rithmetic

The third of the "5 R's" of graduate school is 'rithmetic. Unless you are in a mathematics program, the most "meaningful" math that you will encounter in graduate school comes in two types: statistics and grade point averages. If you're streetsmart, you won't let either of them take control of you. The following two sections will give you some pointers that we hope will ease some of your worries.

> *Smoking is one of the leading causes of statistics.*
> —Fletcher Knebel

Statistics (oh yea)

Almost every graduate school program will require you to take some level of statistics. If you're a Star Trek geek you're probably saying, "Oh, yea! I just love numbers, and aliens and light sabers and all that stuff! Goody!" If you're normal, you're probably saying "Shit." Well, the fact is, statistics does suck—always has, always will. The good news, however, is that you can make it not suck too bad. Although mathematically speaking, most of the stats crap can be calculated with a computer, it's really the understanding of how to set up a research study that is important. If you consider yourself mathematically challenged, calm yourself down and get a frickin' tutor. It'll help ease your mind if nothing else. Then be sure to choose a qualitative research method for your dissertation/thesis instead of a quantitative one (see chapter 20 "Your Dissertation/Thesis). As long as you are not one of the five dumbest people in your stats class, you will probably come away with at least a "B," no matter how little you actually learn.

Listen carefully. *Everyone* is a little intimidated by the first stats course they take. We've got news for you. *Everyone* doubts their stats abilities. Just calm the hell down and think of that stupid train who said, "I think I can, I think I can," and you'll get through it. We say this jokingly, but you will get through it. If you are handling everything else we've mentioned so far, stats won't keep you from getting through. Even the total dumbasses (see chapter 9) eventually made it through. Anyway, we have a five-step method for dealing with potential frustration you might face as a result of the required stats classes. We recommend you think about this *in advance*, and act accordingly:

1. If you are taking more than one class at a time, schedule an easy class during any term you take a stats class.

2. Work on your stats for 30 minutes every day.

3. Set aside 3 hours every Friday to do nothing except work on stats problems. Karl would just order a pizza and ~~Coke~~, okay, it was beer—and just plug away from noon to 3:00 PM (then go downtown for more beer).

4. Only shoot for a "B" in stats courses (You don't ALWAYS need an A, do you? Just attempting to get a "B" will lower your stress level, and you'll still possibly come away with an "A" in the end anyway.)

5. Get a frickin' tutor if it'll make you feel better. It's definitely worth it. (Don't let Fred fool you. He needed Karl's help all the way through. He's just trying to sound smart.)

6. Calm the hell down and quit whining about how useless this shit is, you're just getting yourself all worked up and wasting your energy.

And yes, we realize that our five-step method has six steps. Consider #6 to be a bonus. This alone should be enough to ease your state of mind. If a couple of idiots like us can ace stats, so can you.

If you follow this program religiously, you will be in position to understand what the professor is talking about from the first day. You've got to keep up. If you don't work on stats a little every day, you will have a difficult time during your three-hour Friday sessions. We liken stats to learning to play a musical instrument. You've got to practice a little each day. If you only practice one day a week, you'll still suck 10 years from now. If you don't block out three hours every Friday to sum up what you learn during the week, you will likely procrastinate. This will lead to stressing out—bad for the statistics state-of-mind. By the time the course is half over, you might even be able to shorten your Friday sessions to an hour or so.

Bottom line: stay cool and stay focused. Otherwise, you will be too stressed out to succeed.

If your experience is anything like ours, the bottom five procrastinating basket cases (who would have gotten C's) will end up dropping the stats class half-way through, and most of the others (even those with decent grades) will be stressing out about the whole damn thing. Since you planned ahead and have kept a cool head while working a little bit each day, you'll be cruising.

To those of you who received honors, awards and distinctions, I say well done. And to the C students, I say you, too, can be president of the United States.
—George W. Bush

Get Some "B's": No One Cares What Your GPA Is Anyway

As we mentioned earlier, the other kind of math associated with grad school is the grade point average (G.P.A.). You don't necessarily have to be perfect, and in case you haven't noticed, everybody sitting around you also has a 3.5+ G.P.A. so don't be too proud of yourself for getting all "A's." This is another point we cannot stress enough. Graduate school (not to mention the unemployment line) is full of students who have been honor students since kindergarten. Grad school is set up so that you have to pretty much maintain "A's" and "B's" or you'll get kicked out. The bottom feeders are generally ruled out of the program before they can even get admitted (See Part I "Getting In"). Knowing that this is the nature of grad school, you should now have figured out that everybody there is going to have a 3.XX G.P.A. Take advantage of that fact and strategically plan to get a few "B's" if you need to. There is no reason to stress out over getting a 4.0 unless you are planning on going even higher in your education and you have to get into some snob-ass school that actually requires it. The fact is, if you have half a brain you'll probably end up with almost all "A's" anyway.

Still…don't be a loser. Although not being afraid to get a few "B's" is a good way to lessen your workload and lower your stress level, we don't recommend that you consistently strive for mediocrity and get too many of them. Always know exactly what G.P.A. you need to achieve in order to get to the next education level (or what you'll need to graduate).

> *Interesting (Karl) Story #1: A friend of mine took this approach too far as an undergrad. Although he is very intelligent, he screwed around too much and got a bunch of C's in college. After being out of school a few years, he thought that he might be interested in going to law school. When checking the requirements, however, he learned that he needed a 3.3 G.P.A. as an undergrad. Oops—too late.*

There is absolutely no reason for you to waste your time trying to get all "A's." The fact is that no one who matters actually gives a shit about your G.P.A. If you're into that sort of crap, we're glad you bought this book. Moral of the story:

Do your best, but quit stressing out over grades. They don't matter as much as you might think.

> *Interesting (Karl) Story #2: The opposite end of the spectrum is another friend of mine who worked her ass off in order to constantly maintain a 4.0 G.P.A. throughout grad school. She was recognized as being the top student in every class she took. But, she totally stressed out and went so damn slowly she never frickin' graduated—even after 10 years she doesn't have the "Ph.D." after her name. Unless you're in it for pure intellectual stimulation, don't do what she did, or you'll have wasted a shitload of time, money and energy.*

> *Copy from one, it's plagiarism; copy from two, it's research.*
> —Wilson Mizner (1876–1933)

Researchin'

The fourth R of graduate school is researchin'. This is the probably the biggest thing that separates the classes you take as an undergrad from those you will take as a grad student. Basically, we're talking about how to conduct studies to find out information that no one else has supposedly found before. This can be done in two ways: quantitatively and qualitatively.

Quantitative vs. Qualitative Research

In five minutes, when you are finished reading this section, you will have been transformed into the smartest and most well-informed rookie student. On the other hand, don't read this short summary and assume you're ready to write your frickin' dissertation just yet. Assuming you understand what we are talking about, we recommend that you toss these terms (quantitative and qualitative) around early in your career. At the very least, it'll get you off to a great start by earning the respect of your professors and intimidating your colleagues. They'll be left wondering how they missed this stuff.

You probably had some sort of statistics class in your undergraduate studies. Do you remember hearing about sample populations, null hypotheses, dependent variables, independent variables, alphas, significance, matrices, variance, experimental designs, control groups, factorial designs, regression, correlations and predictions? No? You don't remember that? That's okay. Really, it is. Neither did Fred when he first started his graduate program. These terms are associated with types of research called "quantitative" statistical analysis.

Though we are probably (okay, most definitely) oversimplifying our explanation, quantitative research generally tries to explain or predict stuff using mathematical statistics garnished from large numbers of "subjects." In these types of studies, "quantity" is important because it supposedly yields more reliable results. Researchers who conduct a quantitative study are likely to make generalized claims based upon their mathematical results from their sample population (which is supposed to "represent" a certain segment of society). This is the more traditional type of research.

If you went through a traditional program, you've probably never even heard of the other type of research. It is called qualitative research. Though ethnographers and sociologists have long used these types of data collection and methods of analyses, mainstream researchers have only recently begun to use them. Again, recognizing that we are probably over generalizing, qualitative researchers tend to reject "positive explanations" based upon cursory information used in quantitative studies in favor of detailed descriptions that leave the readers of studies to interpret results according to their own experiences and biases. In order to do this, qualitative researchers tend to focus upon fewer subjects (called participants) with the idea that they can get to know these people, places, or ideas by conducting a more in-depth study.

Qualitative researchers care about what their participants are thinking and why they are thinking it. They encourage their participants to colorfully describe these things. The researcher often develops trusting relationships with the smaller number of people he is studying. For this type of research, "quality" becomes more important than "quantity." How much information can you get from the people or animals who are participating in your study, and how reliable and detailed is that information?

What's the Difference and Why Should I Care?

You probably don't care right now, but assuming that you will eventually need to create your own research study, you probably should. What type of person do you consider yourself to be? Are you left brained or right brained? Are you mathematically oriented or are you a more descriptive person? Do you feel more comfortable with authoritative, "positivist answers" to questions, or are you more comfortable "seeking" diverse, "interpretivist situational answers" to your questions while seeking ideas for new questions?

These questions are important because your philosophy of life will help you determine whether you want to pursue a quantitative or qualitative research study. A person who believes strongly in mathematical answers would probably be miserable attempting to use qualitative methods and analysis, while a creative and descriptive person would likely feel walled in by the boundaries and restrictions inherent in a quantitative statistical approach.

Stimulation While Sitting on the Toilet

When doing your quantitative toilet reading discussed earlier (especially the crap that is totally uninteresting), we recommend that you focus upon the *methods* the researcher/writer used in the study being described. You can almost always find something questionable about the studies you are reading. Since the topic is usually a total snore, this will make your toilet reading a little more stimulating.

Once you find something questionable about the methods used in the study (e.g., sample size, selection, bias), you might not even need to read the details within the study. Why bother, it's not valid, right? Nah, just kidding…Once you find something weak with the study, it really will give you something to focus upon during the class discussion. Not only will this show how smart you are, it'll make you look like you fit in. After all, everyone in graduate school rips everyone else's work to pieces. That's what these freaks do for fun.

What The Hell Is Alpha? (And Who Made It .05?)

Who the hell cares at this point? You'll learn it in a stats course.

> *Get your facts first, then you can distort them as you please.*
> —Mark Twain (1835–1910)

Regurgitatin'

The fifth R of graduate school is regurgitatin'. As opposed to many of the "fact-oriented" classes you took during your undergraduate days, graduate school generally encourages creative and innovative problem solving and thought. Sometimes, however, you will find that you still have to regurgitate some crap on a test. Sorry, there just ain't much *streetsmarts* to that: The advantage here goes to the book smart people. When a professor sets up his or her class this way, just study for the stupid test the same way you've studied for every other stupid test from kindergarten on. If you haven't figured that out yet, you're probably pretty lost at this point anyway. What else is there to say? Better luck with chapter 12.

CHAPTER 12

▼

It matters not whether you win or lose; what matters is whether I win or lose.
—Darin Weinberg

WINNING STUDENT/FACULTY MEETINGS

We've already written a little about how to be proactive with your advisement meetings. You'll remember that we recommended that you always have a plan before meeting with your advisor/committee *before* you arrive. If you need to meet with a professor for a really important reason (e.g., setting up a course plan, planning a thesis/dissertation), then you will want to make sure that your meeting proceeds smoothly and ends in a manner that is beneficial to you. This section addresses how you can make your meetings more productive.

As we proceeded through our programs, we noticed that it often felt uncomfortable to sit in our professors' messy offices. We also noticed that, with the computer in front of them, the telephone constantly ringing, and people wandering in the halls outside the office, distractions were more than a little annoying. In fact, when people knocked at the door (which they almost always did), distractions often turned into a nuisance that were impossible to overcome. The meetings were interrupted so often that little was accomplished and your time was generally wasted.

When you have something important to discuss, we recommend that you attempt to get a meeting scheduled for somewhere other than your professor's office. If you can swing it, try to meet in a coffee house or a restaurant. Let's face it, everyone likes to eat. If you're paying, you'll probably just need to show them the way. Meeting off campus in a different setting can provide you with several advantages.

First, the "non-office" meeting place is neutral ground. When you are sitting in a folding chair in your professor's office, he/she is in a position of power. You, on the other hand, are in a submissive position. Don't get us wrong, he/she is always going to be the one with the power, but at least here, you'll even the field a bit. In other words, there's no home field advantage. You will be meeting across a table, eye-to-eye. At the very least, meeting in a more social situation will turn you into a human being instead of another nameless, faceless obligation. The power structure will shift only slightly, but significantly.

The second advantage is that one of these types of meeting places offers fewer annoying distractions. At your professor's office, *you* are one of the many "distractions" keeping your professor from something else. He/she is likely trying to get some work done, and your meeting has interrupted him/her. If you go off campus, it changes the dynamics. People wandering around the office looking for your professor aren't going to find them. That's simply because they ain't there. They're with you, hanging out and drinking coffee. The professor will relax a bit and will be capable of giving you their undivided (and even more importantly, their uninterrupted) attention. Don't underestimate this advantage.

Finally, food and beverages. Again, this is a subtle advantage, but be honest. Have you ever tried to be cool or authoritative while stuffing your mouth with a huge piece of chocolate cake? That's right, you can't. It's not possible. Food is another "relaxer," and can serve as the great equalizer. We recommend food and beverages for important meetings, even if those meetings are located on campus. Look, we're not talking about steak and lobster, here. Don't go overboard on any of this or you will seem like you're trying to bribe your professors, a big no-no. Your intention for all of this should be to make a meeting more pleasant for all who happen to be involved. Keep it simple.

CHAPTER 13

▼

Success in life is not a matter so much of opportunity or talent, but rather of persever-ance and determination.
—Vince Lombardi

MOTIVATION

We weren't motivated enough to actually write this chapter. Screw it. It would have been a waste of your time anyway (not to mention hypocritical on our parts). But this chapter just wouldn't be complete with out a real Vince Lom-bardi quote—now would it...

▼

CHAPTER 14

Don't let schooling interfere with your education.
—Mark Twain

REQUIREMENTS, OBLIGATIONS, AND THE "HIGHLY RECOMMENDEDS"

Grad school is a world in and of itself. If you are a part-timer, you'll probably slip in and out of this world once or twice a week while attempting to balance it with the "other" world you live in the rest of the time. If you are a full-timer, you will be more likely to "buy into" this world while leaving your old world completely behind you.

While attending grad school, there are a number of outside tasks in which you will be required to participate. In addition, there are others that you will feel a sense of obligation to participate in. Many of these may appear to be requirements until you look a little closer—they may, in fact, simply fall into the category of "highly recommended" tasks. Some of these requirements, obligations, and highly recommendeds include assistantships, residencies, conference presentations, social events, awards, fraternities, and societies. Since expectations vary from school to school, department to department, and are even negotiable from student to student and committee to committee, it is impossible for us to tell you where you fit in within your school. The only thing we can recommend that you do is research. We've already offered you a number of techniques to accomplish this.

Assistantships

Whether a full or part-timer, somewhere along the line you'll likely be approached about an assistantship. Although, they can be very valuable experiences (especially if you plan to become a professor some day), you may not be interested or financially able to take advantage of them. If so, pay close attention to the following sections to learn how to get the hell out of having to do them.

What is an assistantship? If you've ever watched a movie about grad school, you're probably familiar with the stereotypical graduate school student who seems to have no outside job, but ends up working in near poverty as a virtual slave to a professor. This is what is called a "graduate assistant." Any student can apply for a graduate assistantship upon entering a graduate program. Typically, a grad assistant applies for a one-year "assistantship" (the word "assistant"-ship is seriously understated). In return for approximately 10 to 15 thousand dollars and free tuition, the grad assistant is expected to work in the department to which he/she is assigned. In most cases, the grad assistant is responsible for teaching classes (called a Teaching Assistant or T.A.) and/or is assigned to a specific professor as a research assistant (called a Research Assistant or "R.A."). This assistantship is similar to an internship or an apprenticeship.

> *Interesting Story: One graduate assistant was assigned to work for a professor who might affectionately be named, "The Dummy"(see chapter 10). Her primary assignment was to "assist with daily responsibilities" (e.g., sit in his class and correct all the stuff that he screwed up). Was this an important assignment? Yes. Was it a good experience to help her with her career? No. Despite that, this student noted that the assistantship was easy as hell and was the only thing she had to do for free school. "Yes," she said, "it was worth my time."*

You might question whether it is absolutely necessary to go through this type of "internship" to get through graduate school, right? The answer is an emphatic no. It is possible, and even probable that you might end up doing this, but it is not an absolute necessity. Karl did this for a year, while Fred never even considered it. Throughout the years Fred spent getting his doctorate, university people constantly pressured him to "take a year off work and join the club." Since Fred is the sole monetary supporter of his household that includes a wife and two children, this was never an option. But don't even try to tell that to some of the ivory tower types who don't even have one foot steeped in this other reality. Getting out of the assistantship is not a matter of a go-getter type vs. a lazy ass. It is simply situational. Be sure to know what the requirements are (even backdoor "expectations") in a prospective program before you commit time and resources. Even though Fred let the important people know right away that he would not even consider taking an assistantship, and it was not a requirement, that did not stop professors from constantly pressuring him. He stood his ground, they eventually gave up, and it became a non-issue.

Residencies

When going through a doctorate program, you will likely have to fulfill a requirement called a residency. The official purpose of this custom is to give grad students a "behind the scenes" look into the world of academia (like a field trip to the zoo). Or is it possible that its true purpose is an attempt to make your life revolve around the university just long enough to brainwash you? Hmmm. Your specific school and department will have their own requirements for this ritual. Some departments require you to take a full load of courses for a year (sometimes in spite of a part-time status), while others simply require you to maintain a string of uninterrupted semesters without taking time off.

Interesting Fred story: Although I don't recommend doing this, I started my doctorate in one program, but decided to switch into a different department after the first year. Why, you ask? There was more than one reason, but the following story turned out to be the straw that broke the camel's back. Anyway, when I was finishing up my first year (in my first program), my advisor set up a course plan advisement meeting. She was a fairly new professor (fit neatly into The Virgin category) and was not really comfortable with all of the rules and requirements, so she invited other professors from the department to join us. Though I did not have a committee yet (actually had no clue that I was going to need one), in retrospect it seems like the four professors who attended this meeting acted as though they were my committee. Anyway, I would have had little trouble meeting most of the requirements for the Ph.D. within this department. There was one sticking point, however, and it was due to the vague wording of the department's residency requirement. Basically, it required a student to take a fulltime course load for an entire year. The vagueness of the wording should have allowed for some finagling—that is if all professors were in agreement. They weren't. Unfortunately, one of the professors couldn't agree with the others as to how a part-time student could/should fulfill the residency requirement. In fact, you might say that he acted like a complete prick who was apparently bent on jerking me around. He was The Bitch (see chapter 10). After debating the issue for 2 hours and giving it some serious thought, I decided to switch to another department where the residency requirements only required me to take ten classes in an unbroken string of semesters.

Fred's situation was unique in that the two departments offered programs similar enough to each other so he didn't lose any time or have to take any additional classes. Switching early was the best thing he could have done. If he had waited any longer, then it is likely that he would have ended up taking classes that wouldn't have transferred. Getting admitted to the other program was a complete hassle, though. The moral of the story here is to become aware of *all* requirements (including the residency) *before* you get too deep into your program. Again, this might seem like common sense, but only in retrospect. We observed a number of people flounder (and some drop out) as a result of this same problem.

The best audience is intelligent, well educated, and a little drunk.
—Alben W. Barkley (1877–1956)

Conference Presentations: Warm Weather is Important

If you are a master's student, you can probably ignore this section. You probably don't need to attend any stinkin' conferences. On the other hand, if you are a doctoral student, not only will you be attending conferences, you'll be expected to present a session or two while attending. It's another one of the, "Welcome to the Club" activities that is "highly recommended" by faculty.

Professional/academic conferences are usually weeklong events that are sponsored by one of the organizations within your academic field of choice. It is a chance for professors, students, and any other interested parties (pun intended) to get together to share new research and ideas that are floating around within the academic community. They are opportunities to learn about what others are doing, and also give younger newbies like yourself a chance to rub elbows with the (not-so) rich and famous. As you get into your program, you will hear people using acronyms to describe these things. It won't be long before you can actually make a list of these babies yourself.

Since you've got to go anyway, we've got another piece of advice. Once you find out which conferences are "highly recommended" by faculty, wait until one of those conferences is being held in a city that you would like to visit. If the conference is being held in Toronto in the middle of the winter (no offense to Torontians, by the way…), you're not going to see us there. On the other hand, Orlando, Honolulu, New Orleans and Vegas are nice at any time of year. Simple concept.

Social Events

Throughout your graduate school experience, you will likely be invited to attend some social events (unless you're a total dork). Although the following sections might make us look anti-social, we really aren't. Whereas, it can be a great time to network and exchange ideas, happy hours and other social events can also turn into complete Bitch Fests. Gossip and competitiveness can run rampant, and if you're not careful, they can actually bring you down (not our idea of "happy" hour). Both of us tend to be the types who like to separate our professional/academic lives from our social lives. Small talk ain't all that enlightening, and sometimes we just simply needed to get the hell away from academia completely. Whereas department happy hours and functions tend to consist of scholarly banter and discussions about how far everyone is in their program, we prefer to hang out at the kind of places where bands are smashing their guitars on stage and lighting their drums on fire. So, please be sure to keep that in mind as your read our suggestions in the following sections.

Social Event Etiquette

If you really must attend a social gathering in order to network and make yourself look good, here are a few tips:

1. If someone important (e.g., major professor, department head) is having some sort of social event, go to it (even though it likely will suck).

2. While there, be seen, but don't say a whole lot if you're drinking (as you should be). If you're not careful, you might get drunk and end up photocopying your ass—not a good move if you didn't figure it out yourself.

3.   Make sure the important people see that you are there. Don't ass-kiss, just be noticed and friendly.

4.   Don't talk about grad school. This is really hard to do, but try your best. Sometimes it's more interesting to talk about the other things in life.

5.   Make friends with the cool people who plan to go out and become professors one day. You'll never know when this friendship can come in handy.

6.   Don't torch farts and/or hit on married people.

I don't deserve this award, but I have arthritis and I don't deserve that either.
—Jack Benny (1894–1974)

Awards, Fraternities, Societies

Let's face it. Graduate school is like an exclusive and snobbish club. Once you're in, they want you to be one of them (e.g., conform or be cast out, turn into a drone). We would like you to view this as a struggle for your soul. Once you are in, there will be subgroups (cliques) within this academic society that will be vying for your soul. If you've been paying any attention to this book so far, you'll notice that this exclusive club plays by its own rules. Just remember, if you're smart, then you'll keep playing by your own damn rules. If you are interested in keeping in touch with the outside world, you'll need to keep reminding yourself that what matters the most is the graduate degree in-hand. If you didn't care about something before you entered graduate school, it probably isn't important outside of academia—meaning it probably isn't important. Period.

The Winning of Awards: Does Anyone Really Care?

Graduate school is ripe with opportunities to win all sorts of ~~meaningless~~, er, important awards. Does anyone really care? We'd like to give you an emphatic "no," but that would be shortsighted. If you want to become a tenured professor at a research I university, or there is something specific that you can gain from something, then we say "go for it." If, however, your career goals would not benefit from an award (that your future bosses have never even heard of), and you want to graduate quickly—don't bother with them. Don't do it just to kiss-ass. Nobody cares. If you do want to become an important professor some day, go ahead and try for everything and make sure you file it away for later. Eventually it might help you get a job. Bottom line: they can be important, but it depends on your overall future goals.

> *Interesting Story: The "Queen" of our department (see chapter 9 "Other Students You'll Meet Along the Way) was the one person who busted her ass to win every single award the university and department offered. No matter how much bullshit was involved with it, she did it. By the time she finished her Ph.D., she was so sick of grad school and everything that went with it, that she just went back to her old job and completely ruled out the professorship thing she had wanted so badly earlier.*

> *Helpful Hint: Take it easy on the awards, there's a very good chance you'll be wasting a lot of time.*

Fraternities/~~Geek~~, er, Greek Societies

Unless it is going to help your career, blow 'em off. Nobody really cares about it…We both declined our invitations. Sorry, not interested in joining "Me Kissa Assa."

CHAPTER 15

▼

All Work and No Play Makes Jack a Dull Boy.
—Stephen King in <u>The Shining</u>

THE JOY OF INTIMIDATING OTHERS

Graduate school can be very stressful. As a result, it's possible to forget how to have fun. We both found that one of the best ways that we could make grad school more fun was to keep things in perspective and to NOT TAKE THIS SHIT SO SERIOUSLY! We've joked throughout this book about how much fun it is to "intimidate others" within your program. That's not really the main reason you'll do anything. In fact, it shouldn't be the reason you do anything, though it is fun to watch as the others become uncomfortable with their sour attitudes, life choices and close-minded perspectives. Here are some stupid ideas you might like to try:

- Pretend to use a foreign language version of the textbook because "the English version is too *common*."

- Do your statistics assignments in Base 2.

- Email big names in the field (A.K.A.: Bigwigs). Bring their response to class and share it.

- Using a computer photo program, super-impose pictures of yourself vacationing with the Bigwigs and other important people in the Bahamas.

- Tell everyone you're only in graduate school to research a part you will be playing in an up-coming porno movie.

- Get to class early on the day of a big test (preferably statistics), put your feet up on the desk, and read the sports page or the comics. After other stressed-out students show up and begin to quiz each other, look up and innocently say, "We have a test today?"...Yawn, stretch, and then go back to reading your paper.

- Answer professors' questions using hip hop gangsta lingo (preferably West Coast), "Word to yo mutha" and "Big Ups to mah peeps in da house!" Check out the following website if you're totally lost at this point: http://www.rapdict.org/Main_Page

- Tell everyone that you discovered a bug in the SPSS (statistics) software—thus rendering all research conducted in the past 30 years wrong.

- When everyone gets out their scientific calculators to do in-class stats assignments, pull out your abacus.

- Drink N/A beer during class (Real beer would of course be preferable—but probably not allowed).

- Belch answers to your professors' questions.

- Show up with three call girl escorts to formal department functions. Two aren't enough to truly get the point across.

- Take notes in class using a crayon.

- When asked to do a presentation in front of the class, tell the professor you can't, because you're "sportin' wood."

- Borrow a copy of the largest vita in the department. Put your name on it, and proudly show it to anyone who'll look.

- Always refer to your professors by the wrong name.

- When responding to roll call on the first day of class, tell the professor you prefer to go by the name, "Monkey-spankin' Mad Man."

- Play video games on your cell phone during a test.

- Finally, when called on during class, tell the professor that in order to answer that question, you'll need to engage in mental masturbation. Begin rubbing your temples seductively while rolling your eyes to the back of your head. Spew a verbal orgasm, then sit back in your chair and light a cigarette.

Yes, we admit that this chapter was fairly lame—okay, ridiculous. We felt strongly, though, that something needed to be said about this issue. Particulars aside, try to understand the concept. Make sure to have some fun along the way. Sometimes when there is nothing overt, you've gotta relax and make your own.

I have read your lousy review of Margaret's concert. I've come to the conclusion that you are an eight ulcer man on a four ulcer job…Some day I hope to meet you. When that happens you'll need a new nose, a lot of beefsteak for black eyes and perhaps a supporter below.
—Harry S Truman, 33rd US President

Part II Section Review

If you've been paying attention during this section of the book, you would have learned that

- Nobody (besides you and possibly your mother) cares about your degree.
- When in doubt—shut the hell up.
- Networking and Ass-kissing are not synonymous
- You'll meet some freaks along the way. Enjoy messing with 'em.
- Graduate School has the same "3 R's" that schools have had forever. But you need to learn the other two as well—Researchin' and Regurgitatin'
- Online classes suck if you actually want to learn something.
- Piggybackin' is art—not slacking.
- Advising meetings are to be won—not attended.
- It's not that we're not motivated. We just don't care.
- Assistantships and residencies are important—*if* (and only if) you want to actually become a professor.
- Conferences are important—*if* (and only if) you want to become a professor.

- Social Events are often lame. Avoid them unless it gets you in trouble.

- Awards, Fraternities, and Societies are important *if* (and only if) you want to become a professor.

- A good sense of humor (or a bad one…or *any* kind for that matter) is necessary.

You should have now learned enough to get through most of grad school. Now it's time to learn how to get the hell out.

PART III

▼

GETTING THE HELL OUT

CHAPTER 16

▼

It is easier to get into something than to get out of it.
—Donald Rumsfeld, United States Defense Secretary

"THE LONGER YOU'RE IN GRADUATE SCHOOL, THE WEIRDER YOU'LL BECOME"

Even though we assume you didn't read the preface (or foreword, or intro, or whatever it was called) of this book, we seriously hope that you followed our advice and decided to read this final part *before* you got too deep into your program. Otherwise, it might be too damn late. You're already a drone, and you've already done some pretty ignorant things that could have been avoided.

As mentioned earlier, one of the most important things we learned in graduate school actually came from a professor (Note: *One* of the most important things...keeping in mind that most important things *did not* come from the professors). During one class meeting this professor told us, "The longer you're in graduate school—the weirder you'll become." (*Side Note: This professor was the P.P. [see chapter 10] of our department and knew exactly what she was talking about.*) Since by all accounts this statement appears to be true, you need to plan to get the hell out as soon as possible—unless, of course, you are already weird. There's just something about the inherent bullshit in graduate school that makes people lose touch with reality. Be careful, it'll suck you in.

Before you know it, you'll be sitting at a happy hour drinking a beer with people from your department discussing deep shit that no one in the real world knows or gives one rat's ass about. Suddenly—if you're lucky—you'll have an out-of-body experience, and you'll see your group from the perspective of an objective outsider and realize that this is a conversation that normal people would *never* have. At first this might not seem to be much of a problem, but it will get worse—much worse. One day you *won't* have that out-of-body experience. Remember the struggle for your soul? You've lost. It's all over. You've been sucked in and you've become one of "them." As mentioned earlier, if you actually plan to become a college professor, it's not really a big issue—it's pretty much to be expected. If, however, you intend to go back to being a normal person in the outside world, you need to experience a sense of urgency during your graduate school years—you need too get the hell out as fast as possible. Run, don't walk! With that in mind, the following chapters will help you come up with ways to speed up the final steps.

Note the brevity of this chapter—not an accident.

CHAPTER 17

▼

What luck for rulers that men do not think.
—Adolf Hitler

SELECTING YOUR COMMITTEE
(doctoral students only)

Just like your undergraduate (and probably your master's program), you will almost certainly be assigned a faculty advisor at the very beginning of your program. His or her main job will be to get you started on your way. Eventually, this professor may become part of your committee (or not), but he or she will basically be there to help you get your feet wet. Since you probably aren't choosing this person (remember: they are usually assigned), the quality of their advice isn't guaranteed. It may or may not be the best. So, how the hell will you know?

During your first class (and every class), we recommend that you make friends with students who have been in the program longer than you (See chapter 8 "Networking"). As you get to know them, tell them who your advisor is and watch their reaction. The "sucking on a lemon" look is usually an indication that you're currently in the hands of a real loser. The "head bob without comment" look can be taken more than one way. Though it is possible the person you've befriended might not know this professor well enough to comment on them, we prefer to see "the head bob" as a negative comment. For one reason or another, your new friend probably is too uncomfortable or too afraid to tell you the truth.

We suggest that you come right out and say, "Dr. Dingleberry is my advisor, what do you think about him?" Though you still might not get a direct answer, you're on the right track. Ask around, it's like practicing research. Always ask more than one person, and the truth (if there even is such a thing) will eventually surface.

In the event that you are immediately placed in the hands of someone "untrustworthy," our advice in the "Getting Through" section will become extra valuable. Don't worry though, this advisor thing is only temporary. As soon as you can, you'll want to dump him or her and move on to bigger and "better" things. Namely, your doctoral committee.

Never keep up with the Joneses. Drag them down to your level.
—Quentin Crisp

Uh... What the Hell is a Doctoral Committee?

If you're a doctoral student, you will most likely have to select what is called a doctoral committee or a dissertation committee. The committee is usually comprised of four or five professors from within (and sometimes outside) your department. You're still wondering what the hell this committee does, right? Well, cynically speaking (and how else would you want to hear us speak?), the purpose of your committee will be to determine whether or not you are learning what you need to learn in order to be "worthy" of joining their elitist country club of Ph.D.'s. One of their responsibilities is to "help" you determine which courses (and how many) you need to take. As soon as you have selected a committee, they will schedule a meeting to begin this "guidance" process. Now, go back and re-read each word in this paragraph that is in quotation marks.

Not to repeat ourselves unnecessarily, but try to get the point here: Members of your committee are *not* assigned (unless you go to a small school). That's right. *You* get to *choose* this group of people. They are going to become a very influential group of people to you, so you'll need to contemplate strategically. Some of the more important strategic decisions you'll have to make concerning your committee choice include *when* to pick your committee, *whom* to include on your committee, and which professor you want to *chair* your committee (sometimes known as your Major Professor).

When to Select a Committee.

In addition to following our advice in the "Getting Through" section, we recommend picking your committee as soon as possible. We found that many of our fellow doctoral students didn't put their actual committees together until it was too late. Too late for what, you ask?

> *Hint: If you wait too long to put your committee together, you'll end up having to take extra classes.*

You see, every professor on your committee will want to put their own personal "stamp" on your program. They all have certain biases, and they tend to think they know what's best for you (or them). They'll listen to your interests, then they'll filter it through their interests, and voila, you've got their "advice" on which classes you'll need to take before you are ready to graduate. Most members on your committee will probably want to "recommend" certain classes that they think you should take (again, note the quotation marks).

So how does this affect you? We're glad you asked. It can mean one of two things:

1. It's no big deal, as long as you have them helping you form your course plan *early*. After all, that's what your committee is supposed to do, right? Expert advice on which courses would be best for you. Expert advice from the experts who work at the university. If this happens early enough, there will likely be a valid point for each of the classes you are taking. In other words, if you put your committee together early enough, then when you take the classes these people "recommend," you won't be wasting your time.

2. Uh, taking these extra classes can be a huge deal if you wait to pick a committee until you *think* you're almost finished with your coursework. If you do this, you'll likely sit down for the first time with your committee of five people, and each of them will recommend (read between the lines—require) that you take a certain class or two. Do the math, that's between five and ten additional classes. If you're cruising along thinking you're almost finished with your coursework, that's a huge slap in the face. Reality check.

Look, if you're really hell bent on taking more classes, then there's not much point in finishing this book. If, however, you want to eliminate the unnecessary time from your program, put your committee together as early as you are allowed.

*Another Hint: Beware of putting your committee together **too early**, however, you also might end up having to take extra classes.*

Did you just hear the sound of a car screeching to a halt? We know this sounds like conflicting advice, but again, this isn't a frickin' cookbook. You're going to have to do *some* of your own thinking in order to get through. Our point is that you must tread softly. Yes, you want to put your committee together as early as possible...but, if you try putting this committee together too early, you just won't know your professors well enough. And...if you don't really know the professors well enough when you choose your committee, you might end up getting stuck with some difficult personalities. You might end up getting stuck with people whose participation is counter-productive to your goal of getting the hell out of graduate school—soon.

If you put your committee together too early, you may end up with a professor whose objective for serving on your committee is simply to forward his/her *own* career. Pick this professor and *your* interests will always take a back seat to *theirs*. You'll end up having to make the shitty choice between:

1. Changing your interest to fit theirs (bad choice), or

2. Taking twice the load of classes: those that meet your needs, and those that meet the professor's needs (bad choice).

Since neither of these is labeled "good choice," why would you want to put yourself through this? Capeche?

Note from Karl: "Capeche?" Fred is apparently trying to be Al Capone now. What a tool.

Men found that his absorbing egotism was deadly to all other men. It resembled the torpedo, which inflicts a succession of shocks on any one who takes hold of it, producing spasms which contract the muscles of the hand, so that the man can not open his fingers; and the animal inflicts new and more violent shocks, until he paralyzes and kills his victim. So, this exorbitant egotist narrowed, impoverished, and absorbed the power and existence of those who served him...
—Ralph Waldo Emerson about Napoleon Bonaparte

Beware of The Ego

If you put your committee together too early, you might end up having to deal with The Ego. Beware of The Ego. Honestly, most professors have a pretty healthy ego. Read between the lines, we're trying to tell you that most professors have an ego bigger than Jennifer Lopez's ass. Don't knock 'em for it, though. They deserve it. They've already gotten to the place where you want to be. As we mentioned earlier, as a member of your committee, they're trying to decide when (or even if) you're worthy of membership in their elite club. The stronger The Ego, the more likely (and more harshly) they are to haze the shit out of you before they let you into their club.

When we say to beware of The Ego, we recognize the high self-worth many professors associate with themselves. We are referring specifically to the professor with the Clearly Overactive Ego. We want you to be cautious with this professor because he or she will *never* respect you or your ideas, because they can never be as good as theirs. That's a dicey place for you to be. Just imagine how many classes this asshole is going to require you to take before he or she believes you are worthy. Get the picture? Good, now imagine having five of these Egos determining your future—each one trying to outdo the next. Yeah, we thought so.

Beer and Corn Flakes Don't Mix

And Karl should know, because he's tried it. Actually, the point of this section is to inform you that if you don't know the professors well enough, the mixture of members serving on your committee could be deadly. Believe it or not, professors are people too—and these people don't all like and/or respect each other. Get the wrong mix and you're in for a bumpy ride. Remember the egos? We've heard horror stories about egotistical professors who actually use students in doctoral meetings as pawns in their own little petty wars. Even though we view these types as losers themselves, the only *real* loser is the student who ends up in the middle of the civil war.

In all fairness, it is quite probable that you will choose a professor or two who thinks that taking a certain class or set of classes is in *your* best interest (go figure), and you might end up taking classes you don't want or really need to take. That's just life. There is little you can do about that. So get over it. Both of us ended up taking a couple of these bullshit courses, and we lived to tell about it. In fact we found that, sometimes, these professors are actually right on track. It's true—the class they recommend might just be in your best interest. Anyway, we can only give you a set of guidelines, you're gonna have to figure out how to balance the too late/too early quotient on your own. Sorry.

Obviously, if you wait until the perfect time, you will be in a better position to pick the right professors to fit your personal needs. So, how do you know which ones are the right ones? We're glad you asked. Fortunately, there are strategies to do this early and correctly, so don't fret. Read on, Grasshoppah…

Which professors are the right professors?

In order to be sure you are getting the *best* professors to serve on your committee, you'll need to use the network of friends you have been massaging (not literally, pervert) throughout your early classes. Find out who is on the committee of every doctoral student in your program and take good notes. Listen to stories that are told about committee meetings. Some students are close-mouthed about things, but others are more than willing to talk. Following are some questions you might want to ask:

- Did their committees actually *read* their work? Don't at all be surprised if the answer is no. Hint: Sometimes "no" can be a good answer…

- Do certain members try showing off to the others? Bad sign…

- Do certain professors actually like each other? Good sign…

- Are certain professors good teachers as well as solid researchers? Good sign…

- Do certain professors appear to have a hidden agenda? The answer is normally "yes", but some are worse than others. Push…

- Are their schedules too busy? Bad sign…

- Did their committees force them to take extra classes? If so, which members appeared to be sympathetic toward the student, and which were the hard-asses? The sympathetic ones are good, but if they were unsuccessful in persuading the others to lessen the class load, then you need to be wary of them anyway. Do we really need to tell you whether the hard-ass is good or bad?

- Which professor got through his/her program the fastest? Hint: *Very* important! This shows a sense of *streetsmarts* on their part. If they're cool, this is probably the one you want to chair your committee.

- Which professor has the neatest office? Good sign…

- Which professor was the most reasonable instructor? Excellent sign…

- Which professor is considered to be the "biggest name" in his/her field? This one could be useful, but is often overrated. Push…

- Which professor is truly interested in what *you* are doing? Good sign…

In regards to the notes you are taking, pay particular attention to the advice from students who have been around longer than you. Also, always, always, (always!) consider the source. As with anything in life, consider how much you respect the opinion of the person from whom you are asking advice. Don't forget, they've got an angle, too.

As you take notes, make a list of all possible committee candidates. Jot down the answers to these questions and any other suspicious things during the first two semesters of your program. We recommend that you attempt to take classes with professors you are considering for your committee. It'll help you get to know them, it'll help them to get to know you, and most importantly, it'll give you an idea about how well you work together.

> *Hint: As important as it might be, there **is** more to choosing a professor than his or her demeanor. If a certain professor never seems to be teaching a class that you have interest in, he or she might be the nicest, most organized person in the world…but they're probably not right for you.*

On the surface, chapter 10 "Professors You'll Meet Along the Way" was designed to poke a little fun at the different types of people who you might meet while working in your department. But was that really all there was to that chapter? Go back and skim chapter 10 again, and this time look for the hidden meanings behind which types of professors you should consider including on your committee. Obviously, you don't want to go up to a guy and say, "Hey, dude, ah…I need like a "Happy Hippy" on my committee and since that seems to be you I was wonderin' if you'd be willing to serve on it?" The labels we gave the different types of professors were meant as a joke, but you do want to be sure that you have a balanced committee that works well together. Believe it or not, it won't necessarily be the committee vs. you on defense days. It might actually end up being one committee member vs. one or two others—and that ain't necessarily good either. Be sure to weigh the following issues when considering members for your committee.

- Differing backgrounds—read some of their publications and discuss their backgrounds with them before officially asking them to serve. It is a good idea to have people with varied backgrounds serving on your committee. That helps you to resist the temptation of being too one-dimensional.

- Differing points of view—once again, this committee is in charge of helping you to create a solid research study. Differing points-of-view will help you to ensure that you've thought of just about everything. Thus, a sound piece of research that you can proudly show off in the end.

- Do not have hidden agendas (other than to add the fact that they served on your committee to their vita (see chapter 22)—to tell you the truth, this one is more of a feeling you'll get about a person than anything else. Just look for signs.

- Get along well with each other—along those same lines, a nice collegial relationship among those on your committee makes everything that much more pleasant.

- Respect each other's points of view—Christ, if there is one BIG thing that will help YOU, make sure that these people respect each other's opinions, even if they disagree. You really don't want to be the pawn in their petty little war.

- Their egos aren't too big—again, beware of The Ego (see chapter 10).

- They are interested in your research topic—if professors have done research studies with similar concepts, or using similar techniques, they are more likely to be interested in what you are doing. Think about it. They're going to be required to read you're boring prospectus and dissertation at least once. Make sure it is something they might be interested in.

As you move through the process, they're going to have to help you decide which direction to go n. While they do, they'll end up steering you in a direction they are more interested in. If they're interests are similar to yours, then good. If not, have fun spending thousands of hours doing a research study that you hate.

- They have time for you—we've said this about several aspects of your grad school career, and we're sure we'll say it again. If a person appears too busy with other projects, cross them off your list.

- They want to see you graduate—needless to say (but we said it anyway), you should seek people who understand your fixation on graduation. You really don't need someone on your committee who does not respect your time—or your timeLINE!

Once you've taken a few courses and have gotten to see the professors' work behind the scenes, you should have a pretty good idea as to which faculty members you want to serve on your committee. In the end, choose wisely—these are the people who will make the final determination as to when you are ready to graduate. In fact, these are the people who will actually determine *whether or not* you graduate. Incidentally, in case you have not figured it out, any professor who does not end up on your committee—and who is not going to teach a class you will have to take in the future—is not worthy of your time or attention. Sad but true.

Choosing Your Committee Chair (a.k.a. Major Professor)

When choosing your major professor, we recommend that you be extra careful. Find the person whom you respect the most, find easiest to confide in, share common research interests, and share similar outlooks on academia in general. We joke about getting through without having to do too much work, but we're really talking about extra, useless work—not necessarily the kind that results in authentic learning. We recommend that you choose a professor who also has the ability to help you produce quality work. Not a ball-buster (beware of those), but someone who can sincerely help you. Since this person is the chair of your committee and your primary advisor, he or she should basically be a saint. A good committee chair should:

- Help you plan your timeline for completion

- Help you select your courses

- Help you choose your committee members

- Help you narrow down your research topic

- Read and critique the rough drafts of your prospectus and dissertation

- Mentor you by allowing you to work closely with them

- Provide over-all moral support

- Possibly even help you find a job

Once again, your major professor should basically be a saint. Look long and hard, take this decision very seriously, and we suspect that you'll find one. They're there. As you'll hear us say time and again, know what you are getting into *before* you "jump." We recommend that you read some of your potential professors' publications *before* you make this decision. Later, once you have chosen this person to serve, read up even more!

Others need to recognize your major professor's sainthood as well—especially other faculty members. In order for things to run as smoothly as possible from here on out, your major professor should be well-respected by other members of the faculty—otherwise your committee meetings may become the means for others to get back at a colleague they can't stand. If your department is typical, the saints will be around, and should be easy to recognize. Harder, though, will be your ability to convince them to chair your committee. Since everyone can see how awesome these folks are, they'll likely be popular, and their time will be spread thin. Even if you can't find the perfect saint, a strong major professor is highly recommended. Once you choose this person, they can help you assemble the rest of your committee. They should recommend other professors whom they "play well with." For your sake, we hope so. Good luck, and remember, proceed with extreme caution.

When we say that "others" need to recognize the sainthood of your prospective committee chair, you should understand that we recommend that you include other trusted students in that assessment as well. Some typical questions you should ask other students before choosing your major professor:

- Does this person have enough time to do the job right or is this person swamped with other commitments?

- Is this person organized enough to do what is necessary or will you find yourself making appointments that won't be kept?

- Is this person really interested in mentoring students? (Many are not.)

- Does this person really want to see students succeed, or are there ego problems?

- Does this person want to help students get through or is this person seeking an extra "helper?"

- Does this person ask too much from you?

- Does this person ask for too little of you?

- Is this person still current with what's happening within your field, or has the knowledge and/or technology passed by without notice?

- Do you think this person might be willing to help you get a job when you are ready?

We don't recommend that you pick *any* member of your committees lightly, but sometimes shit happens that you simply can't control. Extra careful consideration *before* choosing your major professor will save you a lot of angst in the end. Replacing other committee members if necessary is not nearly as big of problem.

> *Relevant Fred Story: One of my committee members took a new job at a university in another state just as I was writing my comps. Having created a network for myself throughout my coursework days, I had several solid professors from which to choose. Although I ended up having six professors present to haze me at my oral comprehensive exam (the old member hadn't left, and the new one wanted to get involved), the transition was as smooth as a baby's ass.*

Replacing your major professor, however, can create huge problems and will very likely delay your graduation date. Firing your major professor, although sometimes necessary, can be a huge pain in the ass. Make sure you know the answers to the following questions before asking him or her to serve so that you do not have to do it (unless you're George Steinbrenner and/or Donald Trump and get off on that sort of shit):

- Are you going to be leaving the university to conduct research for a semester or two any time during the next few years? If so, what are you plans for keeping in contact with your students?

- Do you have any particular research topics that you would like for me to consider?

- How do you feel about helping your students find a job upon graduation?

- How long do you think it should take a doctoral student to finish the program?

- How many doctoral committees do you presently serve on?

- How many other doctoral students are you working with?

- How much longer do you plan to be working at this university?

- How often do you like to meet with your students?

- Where exactly are you on the tenure track (e.g., assistant professor, associate professor, full professor)?

- Where exactly are your students in their programs?

- Will there be opportunities for me to publish with you in the future?

Horror Stories

Every doctoral student has heard horror stories about committees and committee meetings. Some end up with members who love to prove how smart they are. When these professors were grad students, they were the geeks mentioned earlier who tried impressing everyone. Some committees seem to relish the power they have over their grad students. Like Frat Boys hazing pledges during Hell Week, they seem to get-off on making it rough on their doctoral students. We can only guess at their motives for this, but it seems to make them feel better about how hard it is to get a Ph.D. Some committee members will never even read the damn dissertation. Though we said that this is not always a bad thing, imagine having a know-it-all professor questioning your work when he hasn't even read it. We could go on and on. If you hang around the department long enough and keep your ears open, you'll hear plenty of your own stories.

*Interesting Story: One of our colleagues put together a committee that has to rival the most ridiculous in history. Although his department required him to have five members serve on it, he chose to have **seven**. What?! Why would anyone **ever** put themselves in a position to please an additional two egos? Just the logistics of the whole thing make us cringe. Trust us, it's hard* *enough to find a common time when five people can get together, much less common ground on philosophical issues…On top of that, this doctoral student felt the need to have "stars" on his committee so that his dissertation would look much more impressive. To do this, he actually **paid** to **fly** professors in from out of state to attend his committee meetings. (What a tool.) Instead of having to complete five written comprehensive exams, he had to write **seven**. Instead of having five people come to consensus as to whether or not he passed his orals and dissertation defense, he had to please all **seven**. When all was said and done, this "go-getter" actually did pass his exams and his dissertation was published. But what was the point? The average dissertation is generally only read by a total of three or four people (the student, the major professor, and one or two other committee members). No one else reads these damn things because 1) they are boring and 2) it's only your first crack at conducting research solo—it ain't gonna change the world. If the person we're referring to sounds like you, we're **really** glad you bought this book. As for us, we're still scratching our heads.*

Piggybackin' Revisited: The "Second Author"

If you are well-respected by your professors or colleagues, they might ask you to join them as a "second author" on something they're writing. We placed this section here to remind you that professors who ask you to join them in ventures such as this might be good ones to consider for your committee. If you are not yet familiar with this term it is when two people collaborate on a project and put both of their names on it. Generally, the person's name that is listed second did less work. Use this to your advantage. Unless you're a professor going for tenure or something, who cares whether your name is listed first or second?

> *Another cheesy Beatles analogy: Though he was always listed as the second "author," do you really think that Paul McCartney got less than his share of the Beatles' royalty checks?*

A good rule-of-thumb to follow when possible is to piggyback on someone else's work, put forth your expertise (while doing less work), and still get your name published on the good stuff. In the time it takes to conduct, write up and publish one study yourself, you could have probably been the second author on four or five. Take advantage of it. Incidentally, this book was pretty hard to write, because we both wanted to be the second author. For details, see the out takes at the end of the book.

> *Marriage and hanging go by destiny; matches are made in heaven.*
> —Robert Burton (1577–1640)

Asking Faculty Members to Join Your Committee

Faculty members are *not* compelled to join your committee just because you ask them to. Getting a faculty member to join your committee is no sure thing. This is where your reputation and relationships with faculty begin to play a very important role. We've actually heard students compare the stress of asking a faculty member to serve on your committee with asking a woman for her hand in marriage. Okay, not really, but you get the point.

Certain faculty members might choose to turn you down if they are not confident that you will ultimately be successful. They might also turn you down if they suspect that helping you get through will require too much time and effort on their part. It is possible that a faculty member will turn you down because she is not interested in your chosen topic. Maybe they just think you're a prick. In fact, they might not want to be part of your committee simply because you have a bad haircut. If you end up in the embarrassing position of being rejected, you might never know the real reason. They don't need to tell you. Don't worry though, like a girl who "just wants to be friends," they'll probably just tell you that they will be too busy washing their hair Saturday night.

In the end, each committee member will be putting himself or herself on the line when he or she gives you the final "thumbs up." The committee is personally guaranteeing the world of academia that you are truly worthy of membership into their little club. In fact, each committee member stakes his or her reputation on it. Trust us, they don't take the matter lightly. If they don't like you, trust you, respect you, or even feel comfortable with you, they will reject your sorry ass, and you will be left standing with the bouquet at the alter. Assuming you can find five people to stake their reputation on your future endeavors, then your committee is set and the fun really begins…

———————— ▼ ————————

CHAPTER 18

We are here and it is now. Further than that all human knowledge is moonshine.
—H.L. Mencken (1880–1956)

WRITTEN COMPREHENSIVE EXAMS

Once you have completed your coursework, you will likely have to take written and oral exams to prove that you actually learned something. As mentioned earlier, the grades you received (unless they're C's or below) don't matter a whole hell of a lot in grad school—whether or not you can pass these exams will show your committee if and/or what you've actually learned—and *that* is what really counts in the end.

> *Hint: As you get toward the end of your program, you'll probably start getting anxious. You'll begin to feel the need to GET THE HELL OUT. If you can successfully negotiate it with your committee (we both did), it is actually possible to begin your written exams **before** your coursework has even been completed. As with all of our advice, use your own judgment. Be aware of your own limitations, and be certain that you can handle the extra load before beginning negotiations.*

Although the point of this book is to show you how to avoid unnecessary crap and jump through the grad school hoops easily (or sometimes even walk around them completely), remember this, and don't take it lightly: You are expected to learn and understand some very important concepts and skills. In your under-graduate years, you likely could skate by easily by cramming for tests and forget-ting most of the crap by the end of the next vacation break. In graduate school, written and oral exams will be your committee's way of determining whether or not you learned the necessary shit—your individual class grades will become vir-tually unimportant from here on out.

> *Note: The world is full of grad school dropouts who had a 3.xx G.P.A. in their course work. Do you really want to be added to the list?*

Generally, written exams consist of detailed papers you will be ~~forced~~, er, asked to write. The topics for these exams will be generated by your committee members.

Are There Different Types?

Yes. Depending upon your school, department, or even the committee you choose, your written exams will likely be done in one of two ways (we've done both):

- Sit-down exam (sucks)
- Take home exam (also sucks)

Sit-down Exam

A sit-down exam is one that you are required to write on-the-spot. Some people prefer this type of exam, while others find them nerve-wracking. One clear advantage of the sit-down exam is the time it takes—or rather, the time it saves. If you are offered a sit-down written comprehensive exam, you will schedule a time and place with a particular committee member. When you show up, you will be given a topic (or maybe all of the topics) with a definite period of time to write. When the time expires you will turn in your paper (or papers). You may or may not be given advance "hints" on the topic(s). These "hints" might simply include clues on the general topic(s) or they might be as specific as a copy of the actual question(s). You may or may not be given the option of bringing relevant literature with you, and you may or may not be given the option of using a com-puter. With all of this in mind, you may or may not be prepared to bullshit your way through this. This do-or-die type of paper is full of pressure and can be a very stressful experience for graduate students.

Take Home Exam

If offered the opportunity to complete a take home exam, each member of your committee will assign you a topic on which to write. As the name suggests, you are given time to write these papers at home. The length and details you are expected to include will vary depending upon your major, department, and even your individual committee members. Between the two of us, our take-home comprehensive exams varied from approximately 25 pages to over 90 pages. In some departments, students we've known have written as few as eight and gotten away with it—Bastards!

Some people prefer the take home papers. If you've gotten to this point in your graduate school experience, you've already written shitloads of these—usually, one for each class you've taken. With that in mind, a take home paper should be no more stressful than one of these term papers you've written. The main difference between the two is the "high stakes" involved in this one. The fact that you are given the opportunity to look up more research crap means that each of these exams turns into an exercise in writing. Whether you pass or not will depend upon whether or not each professor thinks your ability to conceptualize and communicate your thoughts in writing is acceptable.

Some people want to avoid this type of written exam, though, for various reasons. Since you're taking this paper home to write, more is expected of the final product than would be expected if you're given a couple of hours in a pressure situation. The sheer time and effort that take home exams involve cause some students to flounder completely. Consider each paper to consist of the same amount of work you put into a term paper for a class. Imagine taking five classes in one semester, and having to write papers for each of them at the same time. Some students we knew were overwhelmed and became paralyzed by the intimidating amount of work, and were unable to even begin the actual writing for more than a semester. Take home written comprehensive exams are a huge time commitment—but, oh, so much fun.

Only free men can negotiate. Prisoners cannot enter into contracts.
—Nelson Mandela

The Beauty of Negotiation

At this point, you might feel like a prisoner—but parole is possible if you play your cards right. Seriously, negotiation (as always) is key to speeding up your impending departure. Depending upon the committee you choose, there are several factors you might be able to negotiate. One, certain committee members will be more apt to let you decide what type of written exam you prefer. If you have that type of committee (and we hope you do), they might allow you to take part in the creation of your topics. No kidding. If you can get your topics to be directly or even indirectly related to your dissertation topic, you'll save yourself a lot of time later in the "getting the hell out" process.

> *Hint from Fred: I negotiated with my committee members, and in the end, wrote my literature review as one of my written exams. That saved me months. One of my other written exams involved inquiry into a specific research technique that I was not comfortable with, but was thinking about using in my dissertation study. After investigating the particulars of this technique, I discarded it and chose not to use it in my dissertation. This might seem wasteful, but it is not. I was able to eliminate a possible research technique before beginning the dissertation process. In addition, I was able to use this written comp to become more proficient in one of the 5 R's. One of the foundations of this book should be getting clearer and clearer to you: Always be aware of where you are in your program and what is coming next. Keeping one step ahead of yourself should help you to make **informed** decisions on what to do now—always with the future in mind. Remember that one thing always leads to the next. Many graduate students spend a lot of their graduate school experience making **ignorant** decisions—some of them very costly in wasted time, money, and/or effort.*

Since each professor is ultimately responsible for selecting a topic and determining whether or not your response is good enough, choosing the right professors for your committee takes on an even more significant role.

> *Hint: This is another big reason your choice of committee members will become so important.*

> *A school without grades must have been concocted by someone who was drunk on non-alcoholic wine.*
> —Karl Kraus

Grades on Written Exams

Typically, there are no actual grades for written exams. We believe that "assessment" is the word you're looking for. There will likely be three possible scores that you can receive:

- pass

- pass with revisions

- fail.

The first two assessments are fine while the third one sucks. When you finally get to this point of your program, you will be one of those old timers that all of the neophytes are looking up to. If you're typical, you'll be so excited about your exams that you'll be chattering about your experiences to whoever is willing to listen. Since we feel confident that all of the neophytes will have read this book, too, they'll be relying on you to tell them what to expect in the future. Now, since you've been such a braggart and loudmouth, if you fail one or more of your written exams, you'll be completely embarrassed. In addition to the embarrassment and stress it might cause you to suffer, failing a written exam without a chance for "revising" it means you will probably have to take more classes to beef up on your "weaknesses." That is probably the worst-case scenario.

Practically speaking, grad students will sometimes feel dejected if they receive a "pass with revisions" assessment, but it's really nothing to be concerned with. As a matter of fact, it's probably the most common grade given. Don't take it personally. The "pass with revisions" grade merely means that the professor actually *did* read your paper and that he/she has some ideas for how to improve it. Put aside your wounded pride, make the "suggested" changes and get it over with. If you receive a grade of "pass" with no revisions, be thankful. A word of warning though: Don't be too proud of yourself, it will all soon be forgotten. Though you've just hopped through a pretty big-ass hoop, you're not finished just yet.

CHAPTER 19

▼

All truths are half-truths.
—Alfred North Whitehead (1861–1947)

ORAL COMPREHENSIVE EXAMS

Once you have unofficially passed your written exams, your major professor will typically set up a meeting (or direct you to set up a meeting) with your committee. The purpose of this meeting is for you to orally defend those written exams. The meeting is called an oral exam. In most graduate schools, it works something like this. The student and committee set aside two hours for the meeting. When all members show up and are greeted by the student and major professor, the student is asked to leave the room. The professors discuss the student's progress on the written exams, and generally come to the "formal" conclusion that the student has passed the "written" portion of the comprehensive exams. They normally have to sign off on some bureaucratic form indicating a passing grade.

After the private "professors-only" meeting, the student is called back in, and the oral exam begins. Generally speaking, it is a long and pointed discussion between you and your committee members about your written exam topics (or issues that evolve from conversations about your written exam topics). From conversations with dozens of doctoral students, we've concluded that the oral comprehensive exam is often the most difficult two-hour period of their experience.

As the student, you are charged with the responsibility of having to convince *all* members of your committee that you are knowledgeable enough to have an intelligent conversation on any and every relevant topic in order for you to move on to your dissertation work. They basically just want to ensure that you have been able to determine what knowledge is important to possess in your area of study, and that you can discuss it with some semblance of intelligence. As such, your committee members will feel free to ask you any question they want. And the questions don't necessarily have to be about your exam questions. They can ask you any question about any bug that happens to fly up their ass during that period of time.

> *Sample Question: "Give three well thought-out explanations as to why a Gambusia Holbrooki (scientific name for mosquito) chose to fly up my ass and bite me at this point in time. Support your answer with solid scientific reasoning and relate it to your proposed dissertation topic."*

After an hour and a half or so of intense discussion on *any* topic they choose to focus on, they will ask you to leave the room so they can discuss your performance. While awaiting your fate outside the room, you might feel one of the following: confident, overconfident, confused, frustrated, pissed (both American and English definitions), impotent, retarded, or just plain unsure of your performance. Most tend to feel a sense of confidence, but a little unsure of their performance (*and* slightly retarded). Don't let your emotions get the best of you here, just hold it all together. If all goes well, they will discuss your performance and call you back in to congratulate you on your success. If all does not go well, they might call you in to tell you that you will need to go back and take more classes. Shit happens.

If you have truly learned the important things involved in your program and have wisely chosen your committee, the oral exam can be a piece of cake. On the other hand, this is an area where a poorly chosen committee can get you, or if you're not careful, can get *to* you. Let's be honest, if you have struggled with some key concepts and simply slipped by in your regular classes, you're in for some trouble.

> *Interesting Story: After several years of taking classes part-time, one (former) doctoral student took a year off from his job to go to school full-time. Six of these months were spent teaching undergrads and taking a full course load. The other six months were spent teaching undergrads and writing his comprehensive exams. After "passing with (multiple) revisions,"*

the written exams were finally ready to be parlayed into an oral defense. This student went to his oral defense full of confidence—after all, the professors had seen fit to schedule the meeting, so what was there to worry about, right? Wrong. During the oral defense, two of his committee members drilled him mercilessly. This was uncomfortable, but by no means unusual. When the committee asked this student to leave the room at the end of the oral defense, this particular student sat nervously on a couch outside the conference room where the defense had taken place. He soon realized that he could hear EVERYTHING the committee was saying about him—much of what was being said was incredibly negative and awfully personal. He immediately feared that he was going to fail, and listened intently for a few minutes. When he could take no more, he got up to go walk around the hallways and get a drink of water.

A few minutes later and much to his disbelief, the smiling committee members called him in and congratulated him on his success. Though it turned out that he passed his oral defense, his psyche had been damaged beyond repair by some of the horrible things he heard members of his committee say about him during their discussion. In the end, this student went back to work full-time and spent months trying to recover from the empty feeling of betrayal before he could even begin writing his dissertation prospectus. When he did begin writing, his heart was never truly in it. After one full year of failing to get his prospectus (proposal for his dissertation) passed by his major professor, he gave up. He quit. In grad school lingo we call it "attrition." Another one bites the dust.

Though this student's experience with his oral exam was negative, not all of them turn out that way. Actually, this is one area where *streetsmart* people who have learned to play the game can get a real leg-up on others. While the other students have been bouncing around trying to sort out what is and is not important, what needs to be done and does not need to be done, you should be able to eliminate almost all the unnecessary things, and concentrate on truly learning your area of expertise.

Incidentally, you should feel comfortable in knowing that both authors of this book passed all of our oral defenses (oral exams, prospectus defenses and dissertation defenses) on our first attempt—whereas many of our colleagues did not. In every case we can verify, these colleagues had taken more classes, spent more time/money, kissed more asses, etc. But when it came to actually learning the required material, some were still lost. This is where learning to *Play the Game* really pays off.

CHAPTER 20

▼

Best advice on writing I've ever received: Finish.
—Peter Mayle

YOUR DISSERTATION/THESIS

So, you finished up your written exams and passed your oral exam? Whoopee-frickin-doo. And you thought you were almost finished? Ha. Not so fast. We told you this wouldn't be easy, and we hope you were paying attention. Seriously, if you've finished with your written and oral exams, congratulations…but, we truly hope you are not just reading this section for the first time this late in your grad school career!

Multiple Choice: Why do doctoral students need to write a dissertation/thesis?

a. *To become an expert in the field.*

b. *To add to the "body of knowledge" in the field.*

c. *To prove that he/she can conduct quality research.*

d. *To get the hell out.*

According to the first stats professor Karl took a class with, the correct answer is "D." No lie. Yes, the traditional answer to the point of a dissertation is to "add to the body of knowledge" in one's field—in other words, to find some new information that others have not found yet—as well as to demonstrate that you can conduct quality research. So, basically all four choices in that question were correct, but in pragmatic terms—if your goal is to *graduate* (and it should be), then the you need to re-evaluate those options and realize that adding to the body of knowledge and proving you can do great research don't mean jack if you never get the damn thing finished.

We will not argue that choices "A—C" are unimportant, the fact is that the dissertation is the one roadblock that a lot of people never get past. With this in mind, the most important reason for writing your dissertation is to get it finished and get the hell out. Yes, you want to do it right, and yes, you want to do a good job. However, if you have the attitude that it is "your baby" and it has to be polished for years, you're wasting your time. Believe us (and if you've read this far into the book then we probably don't need to say this, but here goes anyway), it does not have to be *that* difficult. Follow Nike's lead, and "just do it." Oh yeah, and if it helps you to let it go, you need to keep in mind that virtually *no one* will ever read your dissertation/thesis. Accept it and move on.

Once you have completed all your coursework and passed your written and oral exams, it is now time to begin thinking about your dissertation/thesis. Or is it? Nope—you should have been planning and writing parts of it all along. If you've been paying attention, that's what we've been grooming you for since the beginning of the "Getting Through" section. This document (just like your coursework) has many hoops through which you must jump before it gets approved. Therefore, if you want to get through this process in a timely manner, you will need to begin planning and researching your topic early on. That way, when you get to this point, you will already have a huge part of it completed.

Er…uh…What is a Thesis? What is a Dissertation?

Sometimes the two terms are used interchangeably. They're pretty much the same thing. If you are a master's level student, you'll probably need to write a thesis (or practicum) as your final assignment before the powers that be will release you. If you're a doctoral student, then you're definitely going to have to write a book called a dissertation (still sometimes referred to as a "thesis"). Basically, you will be required to create and conduct some sort of meaningful research, then write it up. That's it.

> *Hint: Be aware that "meaningful" is in the eye of the beholder. As we have stated before, you will likely have what is called a research interest. As you*

move through your studies, you should have been gradually becoming an expert on something that you are interested in knowing more about. Now is the time you get to delve deeply into this topic.

A master's level thesis is obviously not as intense as a doctoral dissertation. Master's students take fewer (and lower level) research classes, and thus, the requirements are not as stringent. Professors will be more likely to hold your hand through the process at this level, and will not be quite so picky. Your master's thesis will probably take between one and two semesters to complete.

For a doctoral dissertation, students are required to perform a major groundbreaking research study, then write a book. In comparison to a master's level thesis, the concept behind the study itself needs to be on more solid ground, the research techniques need to be more sound, the amount (and quality) of data collected and analyzed more detailed, and the final product will be longer in length. Obviously, the length and depth involved in a doctoral dissertation tend to mean that it takes longer to write than a simple thesis. So, how do you write it?

It's no longer a question of staying healthy. It's a question of finding a sickness you like.
—Jackie Mason

Choosing Your Dissertation/Thesis Topic

The most important aspect of a dissertation or thesis is probably the topic (which in and of itself can be confusing because sometime it's referred to as a "thesis" itself). Theoretically, you are supposed to research something no one else has done before. By conducting a quality study, you are supposed to be adding information to your field's "body of knowledge." The following sections will help guide you through the process of selecting a dissertation/thesis topic.

Helpful Hint for Slackers: Although some see this as kind of a cop out, you may be able to consider replicating an older study that was conducted by someone else to see if the results still hold true. Although your committee might not go for this idea, it might be worth a shot. The practicality of replicating an older study probably depends upon the sophistication of your committee and most importantly your ability to sell the need for it.

Helpful Hint for Go-Getters: If you are planning to go into academia after graduation, you really ought to think about your dissertation as a goldmine

of journal articles. Many have made a career out of turning parts of disser-
tations into dozens of journal articles. This is an excellent way for you to get
some publishing under your belt right off the bat.

Start Early

Although the dissertation/thesis is the final hoop through which you must jump in order to get your degree, you should not wait until the end of your program to begin working on it. We repeat: DO NOT wait until the end of your program to begin working on it! Big mistake. When you make the choice to begin your graduate program, there will likely be some natural areas in your field in which you have some interest.

Early in your program we suggest taking a trip to the college library (or your department library) and paging through a few of the recently published dissertations or theses (not misspelled, plural for thesis). We recommend getting a feel for what kinds of subjects people before you have researched, and what format(s) they used for theirs. This is a good way for you to begin determining what legitimate general topics you have an actual interest in. Always seeking to use your time wisely, if you are looking at your department's dissertations/theses, look to see which faculty members served on the committees of dissertation topics that seem interesting to you. You should also look to see what kinds of research the various professors on the committee have been conducting (search for the names in the references of the dissertation).

Even though it will still be too early to begin physically writing your paper, it's *never* too early to get a general idea and begin narrowing down potential topics. It is not too early to begin finding related articles, building your own file library and planning which professors you want to have on your committee. If you are like many of the people we blew by in graduate school and wait until you've finished your coursework and passed your exams, you will end up wasting precious time, energy, and money. Seriously, it could take you *months* just to finish a decent literature review. When you are attaching this period of time to the tail end of your coursework, you're talking about months of *additional* time. Keep in mind, you're talking about paying tuition during each semester you are "researching," and in addition, you are needlessly delaying graduation.

As mentioned during Part II: Getting Through, you should begin your program with a general topic of interest in mind. Then spend the next few years (read between the lines, we're talking about your class assignments) investigating various aspects of this topic. You should do this while meeting the requirements for each class you take during your program—not as a side issue, but as the *central* issue. Always be thinking ahead. Use as many classroom assignments as possible to forward your research. Always think about what aspect of each class you might be able to use in your dissertation.

> *Hint: That's not cheating. That is what graduate school is all about. Certainly you want to be able to carry on reasonable intellectual conversations about a variety of topics, but your central goal is to become an expert on something important to you, something important within your field. Don't get sidetracked.*

In our cases, we only had one or two courses we were required to take that did not lend themselves in some small way to our dissertations. Although it might seem like some of your courses are a complete waste of your time (and some of them very well might be), you should be looking to find a few things within each that will help you move forward with and to help you round out your dissertation idea.

Filing Research Articles: Be ~~*Anal*~~*, er, Organized*

Throughout virtually every graduate course you will run across names of researchers, significant studies in your field, professors who might be able to help, students studying similar topics, etc. Go ahead and make copies of every article you find that might be remotely related to your topic of choice and make notes about any people who might be able to help you later on and file them away for later—you just never know.

> *Hint: Don't "file them" by shoving them in a drawer, a notebook, or a box! Be organized. It doesn't really matter what system you use, but make sure you do it in some logical way. Use file folders, and file your articles one at a time as you come across them. And don't wait until your file drawer is bursting at the seams, either. If an article is even remotely related to your topic, file it. If it's not, we don't care what you do with it. Do not, however, allow these two groups of articles to become intermixed. This could be very costly later on. You'll end up spending countless hours sifting through a slush pile of crap (and re-reading useless articles) looking for something "you know is there."*

Writing Assignments: Make 'em Useful

During most graduate classes, you will be assigned at least one writing assignment by the professor. These papers usually come with some vague instructions. Whereas this ambiguity tends to stress out many of the more eggheaded students who feel the need for structure through specific directions, we tended to see those same ambiguous instructions as license to write about whatever the hell we wanted. We actually found them to be quite useful in serving our own purposes. Remember what your purposes are? Bingo: To become an expert on your topic, which helps you to keep moving forward toward your degree…

When choosing what to write about, you should think about how you can link it to some aspect of your main interest (read between the lines—your general dissertation topic). When you do this, you will find more relevant literature to review and add to your rapidly expanding file library. As you do this, you will eventually find yourself referring back to your own files and thus, making fewer and fewer trips back to the university library. You will begin to see when and how each of the articles in your expanding file library relates to many aspects of your chosen field. In addition, you will slowly become the expert you need to be in one aspect of your chosen field. As you write your papers for each class, they will likely become longer and more in-depth as you move deeper into the program. You see, in the meantime, you will be creating (and re-creating) a paper that is known in the field as a "literature review."

Creating Your Literature Review and Your Reference List

As you work on different aspects of your "main area of interest" for each class, you'll be required to write mini literature reviews and reference lists for each papers. If you do it right, you will actually be writing different pieces of your dissertation's literature review (chapter 2 of your dissertation). Yeah, that's right. A dissertation's literature review really just encompasses a bunch of smaller literature reviews.

Anyway, as you create these mini-literature reviews and reference lists for each paper you complete for each class, you should be filing them together electronically (as well as filing the actual articles together in a file cabinet). The literature review part should be easy. You'll need to keep each individual literature review in a folder (electronic and/or actual). If you're smart, you'll begin with a pretty basic literature review, and as you go through the program, you'll keep improving and expanding it.

As far as the reference lists go, be thorough with them. They're like gold. Make sure that you keep track of each reference carefully. Compile a complete list of all relevant references you have used in your mini-literature reviews. There are specific programs for doing this (e.g., Endnotes), but you do not necessarily need to use one of those. Using a word processing program such as Microsoft Word will do just fine. This may take some time up front (and most people are too damn lazy to do anything up front), but it will save you more and more time as you get further into your program. If you do it right, however, you can keep using (and improving) some of the more basic parts of the literature review while simultaneously increasing its breadth (another great grad school word). Meanwhile, you'll be expanding and updating your reference list as well.

You should improve upon your literature review in each subsequent class, and it will get bigger and better (yes, no matter what the women may tell a guy to his face, bigger *is* better). Each professor you turn it into will provide you with input on how it can be improved as well. By the time you get toward the end of your program, professors who get hold of this thing will think you are the best thing to come along since beer.

Note: We believe that sliced bread is overrated.

Eventually, these literature reviews will be melded together to become chapter two of your dissertation/thesis. In the end, putting together your reference list won't be a huge chore, either.

Hint: Make sure you are keeping a complete, alphabetical and accurate computer file that you should label "reference list." As this book is being written, one of our colleagues has called upon our expertise for consultation and is in the midst of writing his prospectus—too late for some things. Though he is reasonably talented and intelligent, he isn't streetsmart. At a time when his prospectus was virtually ready to turn in for more than six weeks, he was kicking himself. The "petty crap" like putting together his reference list was slowly driving him mad. Not only was his actual reference list inaccurate and incomplete, he had trouble finding many of the articles he cited in his literature review. We never doubted this guy's ability or his will to get the job done, it's just that a little work up front would have saved him months in the end—not to mention the obvious stress it placed him under.

Revisiting the Good Filing System

Yeah, we know we're being repetitive. That's okay, though. Now that you've heard our colleague's story, you are ready for the meat and potatoes. Early in our programs we bought a bunch of file folders and a file box. Any article that was even slightly related to our topics was copied and filed according to its author and subject. By the time we began actually writing our dissertations, we already had just about every worthwhile article highlighted and organized and saved in a portable box that could be carried to the library, classrooms, home, work, etc.

If an article is not used in one of your mini literature reviews but looks decent, we recommend that you file it and write all the necessary information required for the reference list (e.g., authors' full names, year, exact title, volume, issue, page numbers) at the top of the article to make it easier to throw together the reference lists when the time comes—it will also prove to be a huge time saver. The more anal you can be about organization and filing articles—the more laid back you can be when it's time to actually write the dissertation. And believe us, your state-of-mind is crucial to your ability to work efficiently.

In six pages, I can't even say, Hello.
—James Michener

Quantitative vs. Qualitative Dissertation/Thesis

A topic that will come up regularly at happy hours (remember the story about getting out before you become too weird?) is whether or not you will be writing a quantitative or qualitative dissertation. Hmm. Which kind of study should you conduct? Which one is easier? These are good questions to which there do not seem to be really good answers—unless your department makes it abundantly clear that they prefer one type over the other. If, however, you really do get to choose, the answer that will make you look the smartest is, "I am choosing to write a quantitative (or qualitative) dissertation because it best answers my research question."

Then just go ahead and write whichever one seems the most logical to you—the first two chapters will be just about the same anyway. If you enjoyed stats classes then you ~~must be a geek~~, er, might want to write a quantitative dissertation. If on the other hand, you enjoy writing long, descriptive stories, then write a qualitative one. It really is just about that simple. Yes, the real correct answer is to "use the type that best answers your research question," but if you are having trouble figuring out which one that actually is, then use this simple *streetsmart* rule.

> *Hint: If you don't enjoy (or can't stomach) doing either of these, graduate school ain't your bag. You probably should've cut your losses and run before you even got out of the preface of this book...*

Like many of your other decisions, the final decision of quantitative vs. qualitative type of research study should be made pretty early in your graduate school career. In fact, it needs to be made before you begin picking out members of your committee. Academic types are kind of funny about the quantitative/qualitative question. Some professors accept both types of research as valid and important, others pretend to, while others tend to take the issue wayyyyy too personally. Yeah, it's kind of weird, but it's really true. We've actually observed professors getting all red in the face while arguing about it. Personal insults flying this way and that, it can be a pretty touchy issue.

> *Hint: Choose a committee of professors who are compatible with the type of research you are choosing to pursue. If you end up with people on your committee who prefer the methods you are not using, look out. They might see it as a personal rejection. They just might choose to torment you throughout your entire dissertation process. You won't think this is funny if it happens. Now go a step further, and imagine that you picked your committee without considering this issue. Imagine that you have five quantitative types on your committee and you were planning on conducting a qualitative study. Think again. It ain't gonna happen.*

The Prospectus/Proposal

Got a topic? Great, then it's time to move on to the prospectus. What the hell is a prospectus anyway? Well, before you can begin composing your actual dissertation, you'll probably have to first write one of these. It's actually just a fancy name for a research proposal. In fact, the prospectus itself is just a fancy (not to mention wordy) way to propose your simple research idea. It basically consists of what will later become the first three chapters of your dissertation/thesis. As a prospectus, though, it will be written in the future tense and also will not yet be broken down into chapters.

Supposedly, the prospectus is designed to sell your dissertation topic to your committee members. It's almost like going into the boardroom at General Motors and pitching an idea for a new line of cars. You may not proceed with the task at hand (in this case, the actual dissertation study) unless you can convince them it is a sound idea. You can do this by convincing your committee members that:

- Your study will answer an important research question,

- You understand how to conduct a research study.

- There is a need for your question to be answered,

- You have read and understand the other studies related to your topic,

- You will be using the best methodology available to answer your research question,

- Your study will add to the body of knowledge in your field,

Okay. That's what this is all *supposed* to be. Although the members of your dissertation committee will tell you that the purpose of your prospectus is to "determine if you have a researchable topic," the real reason seems to be that they want to see what kind of bullshit you plan to write, and whether or not they feel like wasting their time reading it (to be honest, we can't really blame them). **We strongly advise you to know whether or not you have a researchable topic *before* you embark on this thing.**

You can do this by tossing the various ideas around with your committee members first. This will give you the opportunity to get a feel for how they are going to respond to your cheesy idea, and also to get their feedback in advance of the official defense. If you don't blindside them with your idea, they (likely) won't blindside you with criticism. The actual prospectus will merely help you to shape your topic and explain the methods you plan on using to research it. If done right, when you get into your prospectus defense, your committee will critique it and offer you suggestions on how to solidify your idea and approach your study. That is how a good committee that respects the student will (should) behave.

Many people get stuck at this stage and *never* finish the program. This is another area where grad students who have learned to *Play the Game* do extremely well, while those who don't end up quitting. No, really. We don't have the statistics off hand, but it is a well-established fact that many people get truly stuck at this point. It is our belief that if you learned enough in your coursework to pass your exams and you learned something during your research classes, you should be in really good shape to get through this—but in order to do so, you've got to keep your head out of your ass. Remember, the grades you earned in your classes don't really matter much, it's whether or not you actually remember what you learned that becomes important at this point.

What's in The Actual Prospectus?

So you're looking at this thing and saying to yourself, "come on guys, get past the general bullshit, how do I do this?" At some time during the course of your studies, we recommend that you find and read a prospectus or two, preferably from your own department (and preferably ones that actually passed). Generally speaking though, the three sections that will make up your prospectus are the introduction, the literature review, and the methodology. How to plow through each will be discussed in the following sections.

Introduction. If you start out like most do, you'll start with some bullshit paragraph about the magnitude of some major problem in your field of study. The purpose of the introduction is to describe some big problem in your field. Basically, you are setting up your reader to say to themselves, "Oh my gosh! This is terrible! Something needs to be done here!" The exclamation points are included for effect. You're probably thinking that nobody reading that kind of boring shit could possibly get that excited. Oh contraire, yes they can. And they do. Hopefully your committee contains people that will get that way. It helps.

Anyway, your introduction is intended to justify the purpose and to explain the importance of your study: Eventually, you will lay out your actual research question(s) in this section. In order to do this, simply think of a problem in your field that either irritates the hell out of you (or simply interests you). Next, think about what kinds of reasons might exist that have resulted in this problem. In order to develop a research question, picture your general problem as the top of a funnel—the big wide part. You'll start with a very broad issue, and eventually, you'll narrow down your problem into a "research topic (sometimes called a thesis statement)." That's the part at the bottom of the funnel. The little part that comes out the bottom is the research question.

As we've stated dozens of times, you should begin tossing around different rough versions of the broad issue *early* in your program of study. Do not wait until the end to do this. Remember earlier when we talked about your classes and the papers you will be writing in each one? During the course of your studies, you should be investigating different aspects of the one major problem. This "problem" will eventually be referred to as your general "research topic." You'll quickly realize that there are many different parts to your problem. In each of your classes, you'll want to investigate your general research topic by working with these different pieces of it one by one, or in smaller groups of issues. This will help you to become familiar and comfortable with the overall problem while helping you to build your own file library of relevant research. Eventually, you'll become the resident expert on this "research topic."

Others in your field will probably study your research topic in a cursory way (and you will probably study theirs in the same way), but you'll really know what it's all about. When you start to hear others in your classes talk about some aspect of your topic with faulty logic or misunderstandings that you recognize, then "bingo"—you know that you've finally become the *expert*. When this happens, you're probably ready to move forward with the process of "getting the hell out."

Anyway, back to the introduction to your prospectus. In this section, you are basically setting up your reason for studying whatever bullshit it is that you are planning on studying. Again think of the funnel. In order to catch all of the proverbial water, make the beginning of it really broad. For example, "According to Eatonwright (2005), a lot of American people are fat." Once you establish your problem (by stating the problem and citing relevant research to back it up), you'll gradually narrow it down over the next five to 10 pages until you get to your specific research question that you will try to answer. "Some researchers (Pourker, 2001) claim we are all bloated pigs because our society is too busy sitting on our fat asses to exercise. Other researchers (OldMacDonald, 2002) contend that we gorge our fat faces with too much styrofood. The purpose of this paper is to investigate why America is fast becoming an overweight society." Something like that, only you probably won't be able to say we're all a bunch of fat pigs. You'll want to be politically correct, something we've obviously not learned. Anyway, as you go through grad school, we feel pretty confident that you'll get a little more intense instruction than our cursory one here. While you are learning the details though, we encourage you to try to remember the concept of the funnel.

Literature Review: What Other Research Has Been Conducted in Your Area?
Okay, this is the part that seriously sucks—always has, always will. This is the piece that professors always love for you to write well, because they've been around long enough to recognize that they can piggyback off your work to stay

current. Really a nice, *streetsmart* way to save themselves a trip to the library. If you've been paying attention, then you've probably already noted that this is the part of your dissertation/thesis that you should begin working on from ***day one***. The Literature Review is simply a paper in and of itself that discusses and explains the available research that has been published in your field that relates to your study.

As mentioned before, the earlier in your program you choose a topic and a committee, the sooner you can begin throwing this irritating thing together. Find a few articles, books and/or other dissertations that relate to your topic and steal their reference lists unmercifully. Just like any good idea in business, stealing ideas is not only acceptable, it's the *streetsmart* thing to do.

> *Note: Plagiarism is **not** what we are talking about. We DO NOT advocate plagiarism. Plus, if you're a cheater, you'll probably end up failing all of your oral exams because you actually need a mind of your own to pass those.*

What we are talking about is a simple matter of wisely using the work of those who came before you. Look at the reference lists from a few really good articles, and find the titles of articles that sound relevant. Also, you will want to look for authors whose names seem to be in every reference list you look through. These folks are probably the Bigwigs, "gurus" in your field, and you're gonna want to cite them more than once.

As early as you can (meaning once you've identified a research area), put aside some cash and a Saturday afternoon and head to the college library. Go ahead and find the decent looking articles from the reference lists you're stealing and make copies of them. It doesn't matter whether or not you need them for a class. As mentioned before, just write the information you will need for your reference list at the top of each article. This will save you a lot of time later on. If you can follow through with this one Saturday each year (whether you're in grad school two or ten years), you should be able to acquire enough articles over time to use in your literature review.

> *Hint: If you learn nothing else from this book, learn this: The LITERATURE REVIEW (chapter two of your dissertation/thesis and prospectus) of research related to your research topic IS THE **ONE** PAPER YOU SHOULD TRY TO WORK ON FOR EVERY CLASS. No matter what class you are taking at any given point in your program, try to find some way—any way to use your ever expanding literature review as the final*

paper (or as part of the final paper) for that class. Not only will it save you a lot of time when you are actually ready to begin writing your prospectus and dissertation, but you will receive input from many professors along the way. Although the Literature Review is always the biggest pain in the ass, you can save days, months, or even years if you approach it correctly.

We've known people who wait until after they pass their comprehensive exams to begin their literature reviews for their dissertations. This is the absolute slowest, most ridiculous, and painful way to get the hell out. Not only do you want to have a strong literature review upon your exit from your coursework, but don't forget the "little crap" that is keeping our colleague (mentioned earlier) from turning in his prospectus.

Methodology. The third chapter of a prospectus is known as the methodology. It basically explains to your committee what you plan to do to collect and analyze the data from your research study. Later, when your prospectus becomes the first three chapters of your dissertation, this "section" becomes chapter three and tells your readers how you conducted your study. Methodology is one of those areas that can be tricky, but just like you did with the literature review, you should be playing around with your methodology *while* you are actually taking courses. As part of your coursework, you will be required to take research classes. One of the assignments for each of these classes is often a mock research project. Sometimes you are required to perform some sort of basic research, and other times you are simply supposed to set up a mock study for critique. This is the time to practice methodology. If you've been catching the concepts we've been feeding you, then you are probably already thinking about what we're about to say.

Don't practice with some bogus topic. Use what? That's right, you're catching on—use your *research topic*! This is called a "pilot study." Not only will it be helpful to have a practice run (or several related practice runs) at your dissertation topic, but it should give you some pretty good input from another professor. An extra bonus: calling a class project a pilot study is a sure sign to your committee that you're ready to get the hell out.

*Helpful Hint: Write BOTH your prospectus methodology (future tense) AND your dissertation/thesis methodology (chapter 3—past tense) at the **same** time. You will simply want to always have two versions of it—the future tense and the past tense. You will, of course, have to tweak the final* *version somewhat to adjust it to the exact things you did during your data collection, but you should get the general idea.*

Manuscript: Something submitted in haste and returned at leisure.
—Oliver Herford (1863–1935)

Submitting and Defending Your Prospectus

The way out is through your committee. That's right, from this point on, *everything* you do must go through your committee. Always keep this in mind when you're choosing your committee. And in particular, keep this in mind when you're choosing your major professor.

> *Your piece stinks. We fed it to the turtle.*
> —David Holahan

Submitting a Rough Draft. When you have completed the rough draft of your prospectus, you will first submit it to the chair of your committee. That's your major professor. He or she will look it over and hopefully edit it mercilessly for errors. Yup, we're serious. You want this bad boy ripped apart. In the end, it'll help you. As we mentioned many times earlier in the book, remember to be patient. Your prospectus may be the most important thing going on for *you* at the moment, but your major professor still has tons of other obligations. It will probably take this person somewhere between three weeks and a month to read the thing, maybe even longer.

> *Hint: Being reasonable is important. If you overestimate your importance, you'll make your major professor (and eventually your committee) irritated, angry and resentful. An angry and resentful committee is, uh, not your objective. Remember that you are an extra obligation that is costing them a lot of time. Behaving reasonably and being thankful is expected.*

On the other hand, you should also be aware that your professors may be forgetful or may be very busy people (see chapter 17 "Selecting Your Committee"). Though you want to be reasonable and patient, you'll want to ask your major professor for a timeline. In the likely event that your professor does not get back to you in a reasonable amount of time, you'll need to be prepared to follow through and be persistent—always nice, but always persistent. This can be quite uncomfortable if you are not that kind of person, but we've heard stories of professors who have kept students' important papers for more than three months. They don't return emails, and when the student tries to call them, they dodge calls and play dumb. Once again, be careful with the people you are putting in charge of your future. In the event that you get stuck with this kind of professor, you may need to go out of your way to talk to him or her—even if it means camping outside his or her office.

Anyway, since your major professor has agreed to chair your committee, the bulk of the editing falls on this person's shoulders. Though to the rest of the world you will eventually become a tangible reflection of your committee, to the rest of the committee, you are a tangible reflection of the major professor. This individual will want to make a good impression on the rest of the committee. If your prospectus isn't ready, he/she will let you know. In fact, you may need to submit it multiple times before it is ready to move on to the full committee.

Your manuscript is both good and original, but the part that is good is not original the part that is original is not good.
—Samuel Johnson (1709–1784)

Submitting to Your Full Committee. Once your major professor has put her stamp of approval on your prospectus, it is ready to move on. You will need to make a copy of this document for each member of the committee. Yes, at your own expense. We recommend that you also purchase a large three-ring binder or some other product that will make the paper easier for them to read. Don't forget what we mentioned earlier, graduate school is expensive. At this time, your major professor will schedule a full committee meeting with approximately three weeks notice. This will give your committee members time to read your paper.

Praise and criticism are both frauds.
—Unknown *(but Karl will take credit for it…what the hell…)*

Defense. Once each member of your committee has (supposedly) read your prospectus, you are (hopefully) ready to defend it. On the day of your defense, we recommend that you follow the advice we set forth earlier. Bring food. We're not talking lobster and steak here, just some chocolate and salty junk. The food won't create enough goodwill to mean the difference between passing and failing, but it'll lighten the mood. It changes the dynamics. We don't know how, it just does (maybe somebody should write their dissertation on that topic). People are just happier when they're eating.

> *Interesting Karl Story: I once served on a doctoral committee in which the grad student used this technique. Unfortunately, we still had to fail him, but we did appreciate the M & M's. The fact was that this student's research proposal simply was not thought-out well enough. The failure was obviously disappointing to him, but absolutely necessary. Through persistence (and a much stronger prospectus the second time around), the committee did eventually pass him and he eventually earned his Ph.D.*

Your prospectus defense should simply be a discussion of how to conduct and improve your study. It will likely follow a similar format to your oral exam. Once everyone has arrived, your major professor will call the meeting to order. You will be asked to get out of the room so they can openly discuss the written paper without you sitting there. When you return, your committee will begin by asking you to explain things that you said in your proposal. If you have been unclear about anything or overstated some things, they'll ask you to clarify them. If there is a part of your prospectus that is weak, they will expect you to be able to verbally bolster claims you made. In the end, you will be asked to defend the research method and techniques of data collection you plan to use. You will also be asked to defend why you are *not* using certain techniques.

After about an hour and a half, you will be asked to leave the room again. The committee will talk again about your paper, only now they will talk about your oral performance as well. If they feel that you actually have a researchable topic, they will pass your prospectus. Though they have the right to pass you "without revisions," that is unlikely. If it goes well, this meeting is really a committee meeting intended to strengthen your research topic. Therefore, it is more likely that you will "pass with revisions." This means that they will tell you certain things that need to be improved, although most of your committee members will not ask to see the changes. In this case, you will schedule a series of meetings with your major professor to deal with the changes. If they feel your prospectus is ok, but still needs too much work, they will want you to perform major surgery on it and then meet again. This is what happened to the student in the story above. Even worse, if you appear to not have full grasp of research methodology you intend to use, it might even be possible that you will be asked to go back and take another research course.

Regardless, once your prospectus has been approved, you officially jumped through a major hoop—changing you from being merely a doctoral student to a doctoral *candidate*. This means that you are ready to take a deep breath and begin the real research. No more practicing. It's time for the real thing.

Go away. I'm all right.
—Last words of H.G. Wells, 1885–1946

IRB—What the Hell is That?

Once your committee has approved your prospectus, you're going to have to fill out a research application to the Institutional Review Board (IRB). Whenever a researcher—yes, you're actually considered a researcher now—proposes a study, he or she must get approval from the university watchdog group called the IRB. This is the university's way of protecting themselves from researchers who might want to perform unethical research involving human or animal subjects, or have merely not considered all the risks involved with their study. Back in the olden days, there were a number of studies that actually hurt people. In one case, some human subjects were lied to and ended up being sterilized (that's right, "fixed" permanently!) by researchers. In another case, participants were given the drug LSD without their knowledge. In others, participants were shocked with high voltage, or were deceived into believing that they were shocking others with high voltage. Basically, some pretty sick shit went on in the past that has led to this annoying requirement. See? Graduate school is just like real life. It's all fun and games until someone pokes an eye out. Some dumbass always has to ruin it for everyone.

Your IRB application is your promise to the university that you are not going to kill, maim and/or psychologically damage any of your subjects/participants— well, not too badly. Your university will have a form that you will need to fill out that asks you to identify your purpose, describe your participants, your methods of data collection and any possible complications that might occur as a result of your study. The IRB proposal is probably a good idea, because it makes the researcher think about what he/she is *really* doing—but it's still a pain. We know you are probably frothing at the bit to begin your research right about now, but once you submit your application—it's time to be patient again. You'll probably end up waiting a month or two for approval before you can begin your data collection. The big thing to know about IRB approval is that you cannot begin data collection until the IRB has given you the okay.

Most people sit back and wait, getting tense and stressed that the approval is never going to come. These emotions are counterproductive to your final goal. Once again, never fear—the *Streetsmart Guide* has yet to let you down (we hope). There are some important things you can do to further your cause while you are waiting for this approval. Many of these things are the little details that can get lost in the process of massive data collection and analysis that will start soon enough. Things can become VERY stressful for you when you are under the gun later in the process, but while you are waiting for approval, there is nothing to really think about, so just use your time wisely.

If you have not already done so, you should go back to your prospectus and change the tense from future to past. Pretend you've already completed your study. In your chapter three, Methodology statement, change the "I will blah blah blah..." to "I did blah blah blah..." Also, go ahead and create a separate file on the computer for each chapter that you are planning on having in your dissertation. Begin writing your Dedication, Acknowledgements, and Table of Contents (all the Roman numeral crap at the beginning of every book). This is called the "front matter." It is one area where you will want to thank your committee members (even before they have done anything) for everything they have done for you. Include each of their names in the "Acknowledgments" section and write a sentence or two about how much they helped you (whether they actually did or not). Dedicate your dissertation/thesis to the person and/or people who have had to put up with your shit during the time you've been working on your degree—it's the least you can do. Don't kid yourself. It's really true that you couldn't have done it without them. They've been picking up all of your slack while you were out dorking around at the university. (*Note: Fred put that in there...total ass-kisser.*)

We recommend that you get your paper all set up according to the A.P.A. format or whichever one you plan to use. Basically, you should be doing anything that you don't want to have to put together later. You're going to have to do it all at some point anyway. You've got the time now, and soon enough, you are going to be ~~knee deep in shit~~, er, overwhelmed with data. Get it all ready so that, when IRB has approved your application, you can hit the ground running. If you get all this crap finished, and the IRB still hasn't approved your study, go ahead and update your curriculum vita (see chapter 22 "The Vita (or is it Vitae)"), you'll never know when you need it.

The Chapters of Your Dissertation/Thesis

The following sections will discuss the various chapters required for a dissertation/thesis and what is expected to appear in them. Notice that each chapter should indirectly answer a big question.

Chapters 1–3

As mentioned before, your first three chapters will mirror the three sections of your prospectus. The main difference is the time orientation. Any reference to your future study should have already been changed to reflect the past. After all, the next time anyone else is going to read this paper, it'll be finished! There will be a few other minor things you'll have to adjust, but we trust you'll have figured this out by the time you're actually writing it. Not knowing your topic, research method, or anything else, it's impossible for us to guess what else you'll need to do. The meat of your dissertation, however, will be in the next few chapters.

> *Like dreams, statistics are a form of wish fulfillment.*
> —Jean Baudrillard

Findings (What the hell happened?)

In a traditional dissertation format, chapter 4 is generally referred to as "Findings." Your dissertation's findings will obviously vary depending on whether or not you will be writing a quantitative or qualitative paper. In either case, you will discuss what happened during your study. Did you find what you expected to find? Were your findings statistically significant (quantitative study)? Were you able to detect certain themes within your data? What explanations do you have for what happened in your study? Understanding both quantitative and qualitative research findings is a process that will learn in your coursework. We're not going into details here for that very reason, but these are the basic kinds of questions that should be addressed in your Findings chapter.

> *Interesting Story: We knew a person who said that when he was going through his doctoral program, his major professor told him that he **had** to detect statistical significance in his study. What?! How can a research study be valid when the results are known ahead of time?*

> *After all is said and done, more is said than done.*
> —Unknown (*but, once again Karl will just go ahead and take credit for it...*)

Conclusion/Discussion (So What?—Why Should Anyone Care?)

The final chapter of your dissertation/thesis is generally referred to as the Conclusion or the Discussion. This chapter is the most important, because chances are it is the only chapter that certain professors on your committee are actually going to read. It needs to be able to stand alone and answer the question, "So what?" Why should anyone give a rat's ass about your study? What makes it so important? What knowledge does it actually add to your field? Any at all?

Another very important part of the Conclusion/Discussion section is the ubiquitous "call for future research." In other words, you want to say that your study is important, but that it also opens the doors for other future studies. Generally, these should be studies you plan to conduct yourself. That way you can always cite your previous study (your dissertation in this case) in your future studies. The more your name is out there, the better for you. Keep that in mind, professor wannabes...

References

Although the Reference section of your dissertation/thesis in not technically a chapter, it is just as important. Having to list the articles you used to conduct your study is good. Having to write them in some special little format is a pain-in-the-ass. Although there are numerous formats, the American Psychological Association (A.P.A.) style seems to be the most common.

Regardless of what a pain the reference formatting can be, at least you can get a head start on this stuff and begin throwing it together early. In case you haven't been paying attention, the only parts of your dissertation/thesis that you really can't begin working on too early in your program are your findings and conclusions sections (Unless, of course you're that professor mentioned earlier who apparently requires her students to detect statistical significance). Although your findings and conclusion are tremendously important, the less important stuff can take up just as much (and possibly more) time, so you might as well knock it out early on if possible.

Summary

As you moved into the final parts of this chapter, you might have noted that our descriptions got shorter and quite vague. The main reason for this is the variance of our readers' studies. First, we have no idea what your study will be about or what methodology you will use. You will determine those things in the courses you take throughout your grad school career. Just realize that by the time you get to this point in your studies, your coursework experience should have turned you into a research expert. Our hope is that *Playing the Game* helped guide you through "the process" with some decent advice on getting and staying focused. In addition, we've shared information to help you plan your dissertation and to get started. At this point though, the writing of the actual dissertation is all you, baby! We wish you much luck, Grasshoppah'…

Hint: The best advice we can give you at this point is to spend some time reading the other dissertations that have been approved over the years in your department. It doesn't take long and it'll work wonders.

CHAPTER 21

▼

The executioner is, I hear, very expert, and my neck is very slender.
—Anne Boleyn (1507?-1536)

DEFENDING YOUR DISSERTATION/THESIS

Once all members of your committee have "read" (note quotation marks) your dissertation and agreed upon a date, you will attempt to jump through the final hoop of your graduate school program. This is known as the "dissertation defense." The dissertation defense is supposed to be a scholarly discussion between you and your committee regarding your study. It didn't take long for either of us to learn that their definition of a "scholarly discussion" parallels our definition of an "aggravating pain-in-the-ass". The defense normally takes two hours and is open to the public.

Advice from Karl: Be sure to prepare lots of overhead transparencies containing fancy graphs, tables etc. to show at the beginning. Keep them simple—just highlighting major points. Try to anticipate any questions your professors might want to nuke you with, and answer those questions on the transparencies before they get the opportunity to go after you.

Conflicting advice from Fred: Don't bother with the transparencies. Your committee should have read the paper. If they didn't—too bad. My major professor told me he hated when insecure doctoral candidates like Karl pre-

pared a presentation. He found it insulting. He was more interested in see-ing how the candidate was able to respond to criticism by thinking on his or her feet.

After your overhead introduction (if you choose to use one), the professors will have the opportunity to each grill your ass and tear your study to shreds. Don't worry, it's normal. Though both of us breezed through most of the rest of our programs (including oral comprehensive exams) and had great relationships with all members of our committee, we were both taken aback at how much more critical our committees were during this final hazing event. We privately compare it to hell week in a fraternity. It really has no point, it's just the last time your committee will have the opportunity to haze you. Ok, that's not exactly true, but expect them to nitpick every possible detail imaginable. Anyway, some-times you might not know the answer to a particular question. That's okay. Just be careful not to overstate your findings and if you have to, revert back to the tried and true trick of interrogation—answer their questions with questions of your own. Remind them that this is only one study, but that it "opens the doors" for others. While engaging in this type of bullshit, we recommend that you main-tain a humble attitude while maintaining a professional front.

> *Note from Karl: Looking back on it, and having served on a dissertation committee recently, the dissertation defense really isn't that bad. The over-all stress seems to make it seem worse than it really is.*

Basically, during your dissertation defense, your committee will most likely be looking for the following things. Be sure that you are prepared to demonstrate (either during your introductory presentation or question/answer time), that you have done and can do the following:

- prove that you actually wrote the dissertation,
- prove that the study was necessary,
- prove that your study adds to the "body of knowledge" in your field,
- prove that you truly understand every aspect of what you wrote,
- demonstrate that you welcome scholarly criticism of your study,
- demonstrate that you are capable of conducting quality research (and this is just an example of this capability), and
- show that you can now be considered an expert in your field.

Incidentally, you shouldn't have to cram for this thing if you've actually been learning the stuff you were supposed to be learning along the way. To prepare yourself for your defense though, we recommend that you consider doing the following:

- Observe the dissertation defenses of other doctoral candidates in your school and/or department,

- practice your defense with someone who has already passed,

- talk with your major professor about what you should specifically expect to happen,

- read and re-read the newest and latest literature published that relates to your study,

- prepare your introductory presentation so that it answers some of the difficult questions *before* you get blind-sided during question/answer time,

- re-read your dissertation all the way through, but focus particularly on the methodology, data analysis, and conclusion.

- Finally you should be able to answer the proverbial question, "SO WHAT?"

After they've grilled your ass for 90 minutes or so they'll tell you to get out of the room. There's a strong possibility that you might feel like you failed. Don't worry about it, there's nothing you can do about it now. They were merely doing their jobs—to critique research to make sure it is worthy of being added to "the body of knowledge" in the field—nothing more. After a few minutes they'll call you back in and (hopefully) congratulate you, calling you "Dr. so-and-so." If for some reason you didn't pass, they'll inform you as to what you need to do to fix it. Again, try not to take it personally, just suck it up and fix it. Better luck next time.

> *Interesting Fred Story: During my defense, one of my committee members arrived a few minutes late, and in a bad mood, too. Apparently, in an unsuccessful attempt to obtain a grant (remember, this is what university people do...) he had just gotten off the phone with a member of the state legislature. From the little that I could gather (and honestly, at that point, I wasn't exactly interested) the phone call had not gone well. During my entire defense, he maintained an irritated attitude. Apparently, I was keep-*

ing him from more important activities. His attitude did not influence things much early, since he just sat and stewed in silence—then, when we began to discuss my findings, he sat up straight, leaned forward, contracted an aggressive pose, and dropped this bombshell. "If you were seeking a grant and had to sum up your findings in front of the state legislature—and they only gave you 30 seconds—what would you say?" Without pausing, he continued, "You have 30 seconds, starting right now." At that time, he held up his arm and looked at his watch. One of the other committee members came to my defense and told him that I needed a moment to compose myself. Without looking up from his watch, the irritated committee member answered, "25 seconds and counting…"

Needless to say, my answer wasn't stellar, but I was able to B.S. my way through it. Not giving an inch, he insulted my answer. He basically said, "Tell us something we don't already know." At this point, I lost my composure momentarily and raised my voice, arguing my point passionately. Though I wouldn't recommend this technique (it could backfire), it seemed to work for me. This committee member didn't exactly snap out of the attitude, but at least he quit badgering me and I went on to pass the defense. I guess the whole point of this story is that you should be ready for anything to happen. At the time of my defense, I had known this person for over four years, and he had always treated me, my work, and my ideas with nothing but respect. As far as I could tell, he had never acted like this before.

CHAPTER 22

You cannot build a reputation on what you are going to do.
—Henry Ford

THE VITA (OR IS IT VITAE?)

Who knows? It's a frickin' resume. We don't think the professors even know, and it doesn't seem to really matter. We asked a number of people and they just assumed that "Vitae" (pronounced vE' tI—although everyone says it wrong) was plural for "Vita". Sometimes people also refer to it as your curriculum vita or "C.V." Essentially it's just a big-ass resume in higher education language. Like the dissertation itself, this needs to be an ongoing project. But, only if you actually want to become a professor. If you're not ever planning on working in higher education, you probably don't need to waste your time on this thing—but you never know. We always try to keep ours up-to-date.

The difference between a vita and a resume is that a resume is generally supposed to be only one page long. As with everything in graduate school, bigger appears to be better. A vita should be as huge as you can possibly make it. If you're a beginning grad student, chances are you only have enough stuff to make it one page long, but we've seen ones that were up to 30+ pages in length.

General formula: The longer your vita is, the weirder you are—but the better chance you might have of getting a job at a prestigious school. Trans-

*lation, the weirder you are, the better chance you have of getting a presti-
gious job in higher education.*

To get your vita started, you need to basically write down *everything* you do.
This includes presentations, grants you write, articles you publish, jobs you have
had, awards have won, and other assorted crap. Once again, this is a load of shit,
because you can make a great vita out of dust if you're a good bullshitter. We've
known people who write down every presentation they do, including those
cheesy group presentations that are requirements in many classes.

Like we've been saying all along, you can make anything, even bullshit, sound
like something important in graduate school. You'll want to keep a running tab
of all of your professional accomplishments. When you make your vita, it will
simply be a matter of following a format (See attached Vita).

(Sample) Curriculum Vita
Marcus Absent

Office

123 Kids In The Hall
College Town, MA 55555
(555)-555–5555
absent@grad-mail.com

Home

123 Sesame Street
Boston, MA 55554
(666) 666–6666
fred_and_karl@hotmail.com

EDUCATION

Ph.D.,	(in progress)	Faber College, College Town, MA Music History Research Interests: Philosophy of "Rock and/or Roll"; Cognition in Music; Walking and Chewing Gum at the Same Time
M. S.,	1999	B.S.U., Bulls Hit, CA. Music History
B.S.,	1988	Eastern University of Southern North Carolina—West Durham Major: Accounting Minors: Under Water Archery, Music

PROFESSIONAL EXPERIENCE

Adjunct Professor of Music
    The University of Nebraska—Lincoln
    Lincoln, NB
    August, 2005—present
    Teaches undergraduate music history courses; Teaches Guitar Methods 101
    (Specializing in "Hair Band Guitar-Licking" and hairspray application).

Lead Guitarist
    Motley Crue
    Los Angeles, CA
    2004
    Filled in for injured Mick Mars as he underwent hip replacement surgery.

Graduate Assistant
>   Department of Music History
>   Faber College, College Town, MA
>   2002–2003

Teaching Assistant:
>   Supervised GUIT 101; Baby-sat hungover undergrad students while they slept through class; Graded meaningless papers; unscrupulously dated hot co-ed groupies; enjoyed being called "doctor" even though I really wasn't one.

Research Assistant:
>   Worked with Dr. D. Pheltch conducting qualitative research on coping with pain caused from guitar smashing and pyrotechnics.

Groundskeeper
>   The Vatican
>   Vatican, Italy
>   August 1993–June 1998
>   Cleaned up shit in the woods

HONORS AND ACTIVITIES

>   Grad Assistant of the Year (2003)
>   "Mr. Nude September"—Graduate Assistant Calendar (2002)
>   Shredder of the Month (January, 1998)
>   Groundskeeper of the Year (1994)

PUBLICATIONS

Absent, M. Lennon, J., & McCartney, P. (1998). *A social science teaching model: The role hairspray plays in Heavy Metal.* The Journal of Head Banging, 37(6), 3–5.

Roth, D.L., Van Halen, E., & Absent, M. *Experimentation with drugs, sex, and rock n' roll: Philosophical lyrics and sound.* The New England Journal of Drugs, Sex and Rock n' Roll, 69(69), 69.

GRANTS

Recipient of the General Ulysses S. Grant (1999) for exemplary work in the field
of rock n' roll.

PRESENTATIONS

National Guitar Association (NGA) Conference
"What fishing means to me."
November 26–28, 2003

PROFESSIONAL ASSOCIATIONS

National Guitar Association (NGA)
Fishing Association of Rock and Transcendentalism (FART)
Society for Homeless Indigenous Turtles (SHIT)

*** Hey, as we've said all along—the longer you're in the weirder you become. It
happens to the best of us.

p.s.—We hope we're not insulting you too much when we say that this part
doesn't *actually* go on your vita, vitae, nor your c.v.

CHAPTER 23

▼

'Tis money that begets money.
—English proverb, collected in Thomas Fuller, Gnomologia (1732)

WHEN ALL ELSE FAILS, BUY YOUR WAY OUT

After you've finally passed your dissertation/thesis defense, there is still a load of clerical crap left to be done. This "chapter" is intended to aid with that. The ideas presented are timeless, however, and should be considered throughout your grad school career—not just at the end. Whereas we do not condone bribing professors and engaging in other sorts of crooked business/educational practices, sometimes you really will want to spend money in order to speed up the process. Whether you need someone to transcribe interviews, format your paper, run errands (basically do all the grunt work the professors make grad assistants do), you will find that there are people out there willing to do it for a price. I (Karl) ended up spending almost a thousand bucks my last semester getting this stuff taken care of. I paid for formatting, transcribing, editing and delivering of my dissertation copies to the appropriate places. People laughed at me for wasting my money on things I could do myself.

> *Secret Note from Fred: Karl doesn't realize it, but people aren't laughing at him for wasting money...shh, don't tell him, though. If he realizes that there are other reasons for the laughing and pointing, he's almost certain to end up back to therapy.*

What they failed to see, however, was that my $14,000 pay raise was to kick in as soon as I graduated. Rather than waste another semester's tuition and a lot of my time (which would have cost more than $1000 anyway), I just paid to have it done for me, and started collecting my bigger paychecks immediately following graduation. Some of the people who laughed at me for spending that much money were still sitting there a couple years later wasting their own money (with no pay raise to show for it). Like the old saying goes, "He who laughs last, laughs best."

Just for the record, Fred and Karl always laugh last...

CHAPTER 24

▼

I had to say something to strike him very weird, so I yelled out,
"I like Fidel Castro and his beard."
—Bob Dylan [Robert Allen Zimmerman]

FINAL STAGE: DEPROGRAMMING YOUR WEIRDNESS

At the time of this book's original publication, Karl had been out of school for a number of years, whereas Fred was a more recent graduate. When the two of us began writing this book, both of us were raring to go. Shortly after the glow of graduation dimmed, though, Fred went into a deep funk. We call this Post-Traumatic Graduate School Disorder (PTGSD).

Note: In grad school, it's always good to use acronyms that are almost as long as the actual words.

To get over the trauma of PTGSD, we suggest a few things:

- Throw a frickin' party

- Go on a vacation

- Have sex (stats geeks exempted…)

- Come to the realization that your friends and colleagues don't really give a shit about your new-found knowledge.

- Spend more time with your friends and family
- Get a hobby

If, on the other hand, you intend to begin searching for university professorships, do not de-program. Stay as weird as you possibly can. The world of academia can use some more freaks…and that's a good thing…

Part III Section Review

Upon finishing Part III, you should have learned how to get the hell out of graduate school. In case you didn't understand it, or you didn't feel like actually reading it, here's the stuff you should have learned:

- The longer you're in, the weirder you become.

- In order to get the hell out (legitimately) you have to prove that you actually learned something. Make sure you know what you need to know in order to pass your comprehensive exams.

- If you don't pass your exams and defenses on the first try, don't take it too personally. It's not that unusual.

- Select your committee early in your program.

- Begin thinking about your dissertation early in your program.

- A "vita" is higher education's version of a resume.

- Keep your vita current.

- Determine whether or not it's worth your money to pay someone to do clerical shit for you.

- De-program your weirdness unless you intend to remain in higher education.

- There are two other ways you can get the hell out of graduate school— Flunk (not recommended) or quit (also not recommended).

CONCLUSION

▼

All of us learn to write in the second grade. Most of us go on to greater things.
—Basketball coach Bobby Knight

Although we've spent around 200 frickin' pages making fun of the ubiquitous bullshit inherent in the graduate school system, the fact remains that in all actuality, it is an important and necessary aspect of our society. Acquiring and constructing new knowledge is important, learning to conduct quality research is important, and educating future professors is important. With that in mind (and while we still have our jobs) we cannot stress enough the importance of having a good sense of humor about the whole thing. Those who don't, perish. Or is it publish?

Out Takes

Antagonistic cooperation is the principle of all markets and many marriages.
—Mason Cooley

Just as many movies and TV shows have "out takes" these days (usually on the "bonus" section of the DVD), we thought you might like to see some of ours. Since we wrote this book collaboratively, we didn't always agree on what should be in it, or how it should be written. The floppy disks and emails we exchanged back and forth for over a year had some (not so) interesting exchanges.

Another Way to Finance Grad School

Karl: "Also, don't forget potential inheritance. Although we don't (officially) condone whacking a rich relative for the insurance money, if for some reason you do inherit some dough, graduate school (and beer) can be a good use for it."

Fred: This sounds kind of far-fetched—-unless that's how you paid for yours. It just sounds kind of weird.

Karl: I hope you die.

Fred: Nice. Uh...I hope the part about "whacking a rich relative" is just a joke.

Karl: You'll never know.

Defining the GRE

Fred: "The General Test measures verbal, quantitative, and analytical skills that have been developed over a long period of time and are not necessarily related to any particular field of study."

Karl: You need a citation here, Dumbass. What else have you plagiarized?

Fred: You'd be surprised.

Karl: Not really.

Fred: p.s. Dumbass is two words.

Defining the MAT

Fred: "Blah, Blah, Blah (more than forty words of rambling bullshit quote)"

Karl: You're supposed to use a block quote if it's more than 40 words. Are you sure you actually graduated?

Fred: How do you know I actually did graduate? You got drunk and missed the party.

Karl: What party?

Adjective Spellings

Fred: It's spelled "freakin'," dumbass.

Karl: Where I come from, it's "frickin'" with an "I."—as in "I wish you'd frickin' shut the hell up, dumbass."

Patti (Peer Reviewer):   Sorry Fred, Karl is right—on the other hand, Karl, any idiot knows that "freakin'" is a verb, not an adjective, "you frickin' dumbass!"

Note: Patti never was particularly great with the parts of speech— that's why we asked her to edit our manuscript.

Section Reviews

Fred:	You can write this one (Part 1).
Fred:	You can write this one (Part 2).
Fred:	You can write this one (Part 3).
Karl:	Screw it. You get the disks last. Ha Ha, you have to write them.

The Hairy/Harried Professional

Karl:	The "Hairy" Professional? What the hell is that?
Fred:	I think you coined the phrase.
Karl:	I did not, you idiot. I've never used that expression in my life. Are you sure you don't mean "harried", stupid?—And I'm taking all your stupid "To be sure's" out. What's that grad school sounding crap all about? And now I've got proof that you came up with the "hairy" thing. On page 38 in Part 2 there is a sentence that you obviously wrote that uses that expression again (although you spelled it right this time at least).
Fred:	You call that proof? I was probably just using your stupid term, only using it the right way. Remember when you asked what else I plagiarized? Well, now you know…I plagiarized off your stupidity.

Adverbs

Karl:	And by the way, learn to put "ly" on the ends of your adverbs, you idiot.
Fred:	What's an adverb?

Lame Expressions

Be wise...

Karl: What's the "Be wise—strategize" thing? That's just weird.

Fred: I don't know. It does sound kind of queer though. Dump it.

Kindred Spirits...

Karl: "Kindred Spirits"?! What the hell were you smoking when you wrote that?!

Fred: That was your phrase too. Why do you keep blaming me for all the stupid stuff?

Karl: So now you admit it's stupid...then why the hell did you write it in the first place?

Doozy...

Karl: Do you realize you actually used the word, "Doozy" in here? Yikes.

Fred: Now that you mention it, it does sound pretty gay. I'm surprised you don't like it.

Karl: I'm too P.C. to even dignify that remark with a response.

The Average Bear...

Fred: "Read between the lines, we're trying to tell you that most professors have an arrogance about them that is stronger than the average bear's."

Karl: That's kind of wimpy, shouldn't it be something like this?— "Read between the lines, we're trying to tell you that most professors have an ego bigger than Jennifer Lopez's ass."

Fred: Everyone knows Yogi Bear...Who the hell is Jennifer Lopez? And her ass bigger than the average bear's?

Marriage...

Fred: "We compare asking a faculty member to be part of your committee with asking a woman for her hand in marriage."

Karl: Are you frickin' kidding me? No wonder I'm scared to get married.

Editing... Cutting and Pasting

Fred: This might be better in the "Getting In" section, what do you think? Read it and you'll see what I mean. I've completely screwed this chapter up. It needs to be cut up into little pieces and moved to a variety of places.

Karl: Chapter?—more like the entire frickin' book, you idiot. I can think of a good place you need to move it to.

Repeating One's self

Fred: I swear sometimes that you don't know WHAT the hell you're doing. I'm sitting here spending hours just deleting stupid stuff. Half the shit you write has already been written...by you. To make it worse, it sucked the first time you wrote it and the first time I deleted it...

Karl: Bite me.

Prepositions

Karl: Would you quit ending your sentences in frickin' prepositions please?

Fred: What's a preposition? What are you really trying to get at?

Learn Your Own Frickin' Degree Initials Please

Karl: I would think that if you actually earned a Ph.D. that you would be smart enough to realize that there is a "." after the D also, dumbass. I bet you can't even spell "Ph.D."

Fred: Your attitude sucks. Are you sure you're not on the rag?

e.g.,

Karl: Alright, for the 20th time—"e.g.," has a frickin' comma after it.

Fred: What's the matter Karl, constipation got you down? I'm serious, Dude, I think you need to take some Ex-Lax or something…I think regularity could do wonders to your mood.

Karl: My mood is fine. Bite me.

A.P.A. Format

Fred: We are doing this thing in A.P.A. format, aren't we?

Karl: Do you actually know any other one? I don't (nor do I really even remember A.P.A.).

Fred: And you're the one who's insulting me about being a dumb ass?

Karl: Yes.

Unused Section Title

"Include Alcohol When Possible" (at advising meetings)

Fred: Karl has to do this one. I don't drink.

Karl: Nice try.

Fred: Anyway, it's a stupid idea to begin with. Alcohol at advising meetings? It doesn't even make any sense, I'm taking it out.

Karl: It worked for me.

Piggybackin' for Real

Karl: Incidentally, although I am listed as the second author of this book, I want 60% of the royalties, because we all know who did the most work.

Fred: Incidentally shmincentenally my ass. You are a complete and utter schmuck. You're going to get your 50% of the royalties and be happy with it or you can kiss my lily-white ass. The fact that you seem to think that "doing the most work" is important neglects the premise of this entire book. The amount of effort you put in is irrelevant. Are you even reading the shit we're writing?

Karl: No. Am I supposed to?

Motivation Chapter

Fred: (Call it writer's block, call it what you want…I think we might want to blow this chapter off. I don't have a clue what to write.

Karl: I call it "laziness."

Fred: Whatever. Screw it, I'm not motivated to write it.

Karl: Hey, let's put that in there.

Fred: You do it, I'm feeling kind of lazy.

Hangovers

Karl: "Going to your most difficult stats class with an obvious hangover is a lot of fun."

Fred: Yeah, it's as much fun as going to the freakin' dentist. Karl, are you insane?

Karl:	I see you still don't know how to spell "frickin'," dumbass. And leave me the hell alone, I have a hangover.
Fred:	No wonder you don't remember the shit you're writing. Here's the number for A.A. It's 867–5309. Ask for Jenny.
Karl:	OMG—you're a tool.

Out Takes

Fred:	Just for the record, I think these out takes are a dumb idea. You realize that one of the first things the editor will do is to tell us to axe 'em.
Karl:	What? Are you kidding me? These things are the greatest idea since the Germans invented beer!
Fred:	The Germans didn't invent beer, you dumbass.
Karl:	Whatever. Maybe it was the Baptists.

Bibliography

(NOT NECESSARILY)

Self-plagiarism is style.
—Alfred Hitchcock

Bartleby website (2003). www.bartleby.com (accessed on January 13, 2003).

Bill, S.R. (2005). *The How-To's of Amateur and Inaccurate Cyber-Stalking* Lincoln, NB: Woefully Light Press

Byrne, R. (Ed.). (1988). *1,911 best things anybody ever said.* New York: Fawcett Columbine.

Caddyshack. Dir. H. Ramis. [Film]. Warner Studios,1980.

Callmee, V. (2004). *Koo Koo Koo Koo Koo Koo Koo Koo.* Toronto: Hoser Press.

Candidate Information Booklet (2002). The Psychological Corporation, online <http://www.hbtpc.com/mat (accessed on May 28, 2005).

Chil-Outdude, P. U. (1999). *Life sucks and then you die.* Half Court Press: Springfield, MA

Donn, H. O. (1993). *The secret of life: Making a molehill out of a mountain.* Hang Ten Press, Maui, HI.

Faulkner, J (2004). *Speak English or Die.* Virginia Beach, VA: WTF Press

Frank, F., Stein, K., & Dre, D. (2005). *Battle Rappin'* San Francisco: West Coast Press

Freektout-Bee-otch, M. B. (2002) *Making a mountain out of a molehill.* Fembötte Press: Boulder, CO.

Goode, K.A. (2005). *You Be Da Goodes!* Bristol, CT: Couple-a-Tools Press

Graduate Management Admissions Council (2004). Online: <http://www.mba.com/mba/TaketheGMAT> (accessed on June 1, 2005)

GRE website (2003). www.gre.org. (accessed on November 12, 2003).

Harcourt Assessment Company (2003). *Miller Analogies Test.* Harcourt Educational Management. [Online] http://www.hbtpc.com/mat/. (accessed on September 10, 2003).

Iceoffagus, G. G. (2002). *You can't bullshit a bullshitter.* Cowchip Press: Cheyenne, WY.

MacDonald, R. D. (2002). *Styrofood: It melts in your mouth, not in your hands.* Tree Hugger Press: San Francisco, CA.

Knutz, I. M. (1991). *They're coming to take me away: Ha ha ho ho he he.* Shrink Press: Lahlahland, UT.

Oedipus, H. R. (1895). *Complex Rationalization: Why killing your father to marry your mother is messed up.* Full Court Press: Springfield, MA.

Palmer, N. (2005). *Pretending to Have Content.* Clueless, AL: Completely Random Press.

Palmer, N. (2005). *Why People Think that Bill Sr. and I Are the Same Guy.* Clueless, AL: Completely Random Press.

Peters, R. L. (1997). *Getting What You Came For: the smart student's guide to earning a Master's or Ph.D.* Farrar, Straus and Giroux: New York.

Petras, R and Petras, K. (2003). *The 365 stupidest things ever said: Page-a-Day Calendar.* New York: Workman Publishing.

Rush: A test for echoes. (2003). http://www.students.yorku.ca/~mcdonald/ (accessed on November 12, 2003).

Shi-thead, I. B. (2000). *How to bullshit a bullshitter.* Lee Press: On Nails, NJ.

Shrek. Dir. A. Adamson & S. Marshall. [Film]. Dreamworks, 2001.

Stankey, H. O. (2002). *Piled Higher and Deeper: Who really gives a rat's ass about Vygotsky, Einstein and Mozart?* Bench Press: Berlin, Germany.

Stein, K. & Frank, F. (2001). *Beer: It's not just for breakfast anymore.* Freedom of the Press: Philadelphia, PA.

The Shining. Dir. S. Kubrick. [Film]. Warner Brothers, 1980.

USNews.com. (2003). www.usnews.
com/usnews/edu/grad/rankings/rankindex.htm (accessed on November 12, 2003).

978-0-595-30486-8
0-595-30486-9

Made in the USA
Lexington, KY
05 June 2012